The Self-Coaching Sales Framework

The Self-Coaching Sales Framework

How to Gain and Sustain Sales Excellence

Tom Cairns

BEP

BUSINESS EXPERT PRESS

Leader in applied, concise business books

The Self-Coaching Sales Framework:
How to Gain and Sustain Sales Excellence

Copyright © Business Expert Press, LLC, 2025

Cover design by Charlene Kronstedt

Interior design by Exeter Premedia Services Private Ltd., Chennai, India

First published in 2025 by
Business Expert Press, LLC
222 East 46th Street, New York, NY 10017
www.businessexpertpress.com

ISBN-13: 978-1-63742-816-0 (paperback)
ISBN-13: 978-1-63742-817-7 (e-book)

Business Expert Press Selling and Sales Force Management Collection

First edition: 2025

10 9 8 7 6 5 4 3 2 1

EU SAFETY REPRESENTATIVE
Mare Nostrum Group B.V.
Mauritskade 21D
1091 GC Amsterdam
The Netherlands
gpsr@mare-nostrum.co.uk

For Paula

Description

To survive and thrive in the business of sales today you need to know how to deliver predictable, repeatable, consistent sales results in our unpredictable, interactive, connected AI-automated world. Knowing what to do and why you are doing it is important, but knowing *how* to apply that knowledge is critical.

This book describes and demonstrates how to improve the hard sales skills, such as business planning, prospecting, insight, and progression, and combine them with the soft skills, such as critical thinking, problem-solving, creativity, originality, and strategizing.

Building on decades of sales executive management know-how, coaching practice, and research, the author details how to apply an easy-to-use, practical methodology that will differentiate you from the crowd. Applied to real-world examples and case studies, the framework equips anyone in sales, management, or sales support with practical and proven unique sales tools and powerful hands-on sales techniques.

Digital links within the book allow downloading of techniques and tools to practice on sales opportunities. **This book transforms hard working, must do better, nearly on target salespeople into smart working, high achieving, always on target sales professionals who will survive and thrive.**

Contents

Testimonials

"Tom is the acknowledged master of consistently winning large, complex deals. For the first time, he shares all his concepts and the processes he follows. Whether you are just starting out in enterprise class B2B sales, or just want to win more of them, this is THE book for you. Packed with ideas, tools, techniques and best processes, this is a masterclass in winning those critical deals. This book is gold–highly recommended."—**Jim Irving, multiaward winning author of the *B2B Selling Guidebook* series**

"Tom Cairns provides a step-by-step guide underpinned by personal experience, numerous case studies, and practical exercises, including how to adapt to AI. This book is essential for everyone from starters to experienced sales practitioners. You'll never view selling in the same way again. Good stuff and strongly recommended!" —**Tony Boobier, *AI and Analytics* author**

"Tom Cairns has been one of my main go-to advisors for sales and deal coaching for over fifteen years. He brings a practical and easy to implement methodology to the sales process, all supported by easy to understand and straight forward tools that help any seller or sales leader improve their productivity and win rates. I was thrilled when I heard Tom was planning to share his expertise with a wider audience. I recommend this book to anyone that is looking to uplevel their sales efforts."—**Greg Adams, Global Technology Executive and former Enterprise Sales Leader**

"This book is the ultimate guide to ensure your consistent growth and career success especially in the world of complex, high-value sales. Step-by-step, and so practical. Highly recommended."—**Jonathan Ellard, Business Development Director**

"Working with Tom, and using his tools, is a fundamental part of being successful in sales. His coaching can be credited with my sales success and that of

my teams. I wouldn't have experienced the successes I've had if it wasn't for the tools and techniques in this book."—**Steven Lockwood, VP Sales UKI**

"*Tom has nailed it with this book and program. A must read for anyone who wants to accelerate their sales success.*"—**Bob Evans, Director, EMEA Partners and Alliances**

Introduction

The interaction between a professional salesperson, multiple stakeholders, and buyers in a business looking to purchase a solution to their business problem is complex and is not a straightforward sequential process. Sales leaders know that a good solution with a great sales team tends to beat a great solution with a poor sales team. Sales excellence and high-performance matter and are the key ingredients in creating a great sales team.

Over the last 20 years, the sales process has been automated with ever-advancing customer relationship (CRM) systems. In the last five years, artificial intelligence (AI) has made rapid inroads into sales automation and promises great leaps in technology to combine with CRM systems and support sales and the sales professional now and into the future. Any process that can be automated will be, and then integrated into all company business systems.

Alongside these technological developments, there are hundreds of publications every year that describe the latest proven sales processes and methodologies to guarantee sales success. As a successful professional salesperson, manager, senior executive, and sales coach, I have probably read most of them. Many of the ideas and methods are excellent. Many are not. I have implemented the best of them into my own approach and career. However, there remains one nagging problem that keeps popping up. The most popular ideas cover why you do it and comprehensively describe what you need to do, but very rarely do they adequately cover how you do it in that unique complex interaction between the salesperson, the stakeholders, and the buyers. I find the how missing from most of the methodologies and processes. Many of the senior managers and salespeople I have worked with seem to agree. In my executive sales management career and my recent coaching activities, I am often asked this question. I have invested in the latest sales training, ensured my sales managers have read and applied the methods in the latest hot sales book, and implemented the latest CRM and AI tools, so why, after all this investment of time and money, are my salespeople win rates not improved, the sales forecasts often wrong, and the sales revenue not as we planned?

To answer that question and provide a solution after deep research combined with my 40 years of experience and then hundreds of coaching workshops attended by thousands of salespeople and managers, I developed a simple, hassle-free, self-coaching, practical methodology and framework. Over 4,500 salespeople surveyed after attending my sales coaching workshops over the last 14 years report a significant improvement in their sales success and win rates. Hundreds of top managers have agreed, as you can see on my website; details are in the appendix. Today, many of the individual salespeople who I coach personally every week tell me how they successfully apply the sales techniques, tools, and self-coaching framework to their ongoing sales deals and, as a result, have significantly increased and improved their win rate, sales forecasts, and sales revenue.

CRM systems growth, sales process automation, and now AI maturity have changed the sales world and the business world more in the last 15 years than in the previous 100 years. However, the golden rule of GIGO must be followed. "Garbage In" means "Garbage Out" (GIGO) which means that if the data going into your systems is incorrect and has errors, then everything that follows is incorrect and has errors. For example, your hot deal just slipped into next quarter, your definite sale has been lost, your sales forecasts did not happen, and you were overambitious and just plain wrong. Consequently, your boss is not happy, nor is your boss' boss, all the way up to the executives who cannot effectively manage their company if the sales forecasts are always incorrect. This applies to all systems but especially CRMs, sales automation, and AI.

In a recent survey by SugarCRM, when executives were asked their top priorities for maximizing the value of their CRM platform over the next five years, the number two response was using AI, behind a complete view of customer interactions. The next generation of generative AI is proving to be a key driver of personalized engagement, content creation, and more customer-centric decision making. Remember, AI is *not* a decision-making tool. It is a decision-support tool to help better decision making. Humans still must make the decisions. A recent article in *Harvard Business Review* in March 2023 states that sales is primed to quickly become a leading adopter of generative AI, the form of AI used by OpenAI (the company behind ChatGPT) and its competitors. AI-powered systems are on the way to becoming every salesperson's (and every sales manager's) indispensable digital assistant. The important word here is assistant. AI is an important support sales tool, but it will not replace sales skills and techniques, nor will it automatically transform a sales professional's average results and performance into sales excellence and high performance. That requires unique human skills.

The types of questions you ask Artificial Intelligence Systems are critical because AI will support your efforts. When you ask the right question, then AI rewards you with the right answer. Asking the wrong questions will result in the wrong answer. Because AI does not have the capability to make decisions for you, if your decisions and actions are based on incorrect answers from AI and your CRM systems contain data errors and mistakes, the wrong data will drive the wrong questions, which will result in the wrong answers. The knowledge gained from these automated systems is increasingly important to provide the day-to-day actions of "what" and "why" you do an action, and that knowledge and data must be accurate. CRMs are developing rapidly, combining with AI to make the process of selling much more informed and efficient. You still need the ability to apply that knowledge to act and make the right decisions with your prospective customer to help solve their business problems and achieve their desired business outcomes.

To be more effective and successful is the goal of any sales team, and it is much more important and critical to your success to know "how" to execute that knowledge once it is filtered and checked for accuracy. That is the critical skill in creating sales excellence.

The focus of this book is to provide the practical capability and methodologies to guarantee the accuracy of data input combined with the right skill set to gain and sustain sales excellence.

The outcome of applying the techniques and tools will be to provide you with a methodology to gain and sustain the capability to create and apply your personal, unique, bespoke, and effective sales approach. This is critical and will help you to capitalize and go beyond your CRM to achieve predictable, repeatable sales excellence in the unpredictable, interactive, connected world of business today. The result will help you as an individual salesperson create high performance, and as a manager, it will help you to create and build great sales teams who excel in all sales skills to produce consistent, reliable, and predictable results.

The Background to how and why This Book Was Developed

During my 46 years in sales as a company executive leader, sales manager, and salesperson, which includes six years as an international B2B sales coach with IBM, a global leader in technology, and the last eight years as an independent sales coach, many people in the business of sales have often said to me they want and need:

- A simple, hassle-free, effective, proven methodology that increases the sales team's productivity by delivering immediate and real returns on the recent and ongoing investments in CRM, sales automation, and AI. The desired result required by company executives is to make the sales process easier, repeatable, and predictable in an unpredictable world. In addition, it delivers accurate forecasts every time, reduces administration, saves time, and crucially has been proven to help gain and sustain sales revenue growth.
- Effective tools and techniques that act as a bolt-on to your CRM, providing an extra filter of sales data to ensure the accuracy of that data input and thus increase sales forecast accuracy, results, and sales productivity.
- A reliable, evidence-based method that checks sales processes align with customer buying processes to get sales back in sync with buyers and desired business outcomes.
- A sales progression tool that accurately measures and quantifies the probability of sales success to deliver the desired business outcomes that customers really value and trust and want to repeat.
- A cadence and review process on sales opportunities that guarantees forecasted sales are progressed, accurate, and on the right track all the time to deliver consistent sales.

- A bespoke self-coaching guide that simply describes the required sales activities, checks progress, highlights milestones, and provides practical sales execution tools.

So I felt driven to help all sales teams achieve their goals. I am writing this book because I created and provided proven tools, techniques, frameworks, and methodologies that seemed to meet and satisfy the above needs of sales executives, sales organizations, sales managers, and sales teams. Digging deep into research combined with my experience, plus providing real-world examples and case studies, I believe the tools and techniques helped many sales organizations and sales individuals achieve their business and personal goals. I continue to coach sales teams every day applying this methodology to help create predictable, repeatable, and outstanding sales results. Many colleagues urged me to create a book that would combine my coaching activity and methodology and provide a vehicle for a wider audience who may then benefit and become more successful in business and in life. I want to share and inform, teach and train, coach, and develop sales excellence techniques to help organizations succeed in our big data, dynamically constantly changing sales automation, and AI business world. That is the purpose of this book. I do hope you enjoy it.

How to Use This Book and Gain Maximum Return From Your Investment.

Sales is not and never has been a sequential process that you slavishly must follow. It is an interactive process that often has numerous starts and stops, back and forward, depending on the dynamic and constantly changing needs of the customers. Consequently, this book is designed interactively so that the reader can jump from chapter to chapter or to relevant sections that they feel interest them or topics where they feel they need immediate help and improvement. To help the reader navigate the contents and get the best out of the book for their own personal needs, the book is divided into chapters that clearly highlight individual skills that need to be learned and how to practice gaining sales excellence in today's business world. The concluding chapter focuses on how to sustain that excellence and be consistent.

However, if you are impatient like me and like to go to the end of a book first to see the conclusion and outcomes, then I recommend reading and rereading the final Chapter 11 and the conclusion since they pull all the content together and explain how to immediately apply the framework and methodology. Chapter 2 identifies and describes how to improve the eight key sales skills. I think you will then want to investigate Chapters 3 to 10, which describe in detail how to use the specific tools and techniques to achieve improvement and excellence in each sales skill set. The chapters can be read in any sequence depending on your needs and expertise.

Finally, to help the learning process and as a thank you for purchasing and reading this book, the Appendix explains how you can contact me and gain a special one-off discount voucher code that you can use to download *The Sales Excellence Framework* at a special price from my website www.salestechnique.com.

In the Appendix, there is also a helpful guide to navigate your way around the sales excellence methodology, tools, and techniques.

I have added a list of key references cited in Chapter 1. I have also added a combined bibliography and a suggested reading list. I urge you to read the books that interest you because the secret of success in anything is to always be learning. I have found many of these books taught me important concepts and helped continue to refresh my learning and knowledge.

Should you need my personal help, then contact me via my email at tom@salestechnique.com, and I wish you good selling that rewards you with happy customers.

CHAPTER 1

How Artificial Intelligence and New Technological Developments Are Changing the Role of Sales

Is Artificial Intelligence (AI) as Important and as Everyone Is Saying?

Max Tegmark, in his book *Life 3.0*, starts his first chapter with a quote from the Future of Life Institute, of which he is a cofounder, saying that technology is giving the potential for humans to flourish like never before, or to self-destruct.[1] Tegmark describes AI technology as requiring the most important conversation of our time. Many AI experts and commentators believe that we stand at the beginning of a new era. What was once science fiction is fast becoming reality, as AI transforms everything, even our very sense of what it means to be human. More than any previous technology AI has the potential to revolutionize our future in business and society. In the sales profession, AI is now being adopted rapidly and is catching up with marketing, which has already adopted many of the new AI programs available, replacing many people and processes over the last five years. Any process that can be automated will be, especially if costs can be reduced. However, most experts also agree that AI is a decision-support technology for humans and not a decision-making technology that will replace humans. Tegmark and others believe that AI may well develop into a decision-making technology in areas where humans are not required, but worry that while AI will help life and business flourish, it will eventually outsmart us all and may even replace humans altogether. However, they also believe that where human behavior and innovation are critical to success those skill areas will flourish in parallel with the march of AI technology. Sales is a uniquely human activity, especially in large-value complex deals. All sales revenue in these areas comes mainly through human effort applying innovative, original, and unique skills. In the buying cycle, humans tend to be illogical and irrational. Consequently, sales will certainly adopt and change significantly due to new technology and AI, but there will be core areas where unique human skills are required to survive and flourish. This book and the methodology applied highlight how to achieve predictable sales success in an automated unpredictable world.

What Are Sales and Selling?

Before we start looking at how new technology, AI, and automation are impacting the role of sales and selling, it might be worth spending a few moments on understanding sales and selling. In his great book *To Sell is Human*, Daniel H. Pink,[2] a renowned social psychologist and the author of five *New York Times* bestsellers, summed up for me the best definition of sales, which I believe still holds true today. He said that selling is the ability to move others to exchange what they have for what we have. Basically, it is the ability to trade. This ability has been essential to humanity's survival since the beginning of the evolution of our species, *Homo Sapiens*. This ability to sell and therefore trade is critical to our survival and happiness, and so he concluded that the ability to sell is fundamentally human. We all must sell and trade something to survive and prosper, and if we fail in this human skill, then we fail to survive in any culture and fail to find happiness and fulfillment in our lives. He believes the advent of new technology and social media is becoming an even more important skill. In fact, he states we are all in sales now.

Technology and automation have taken over most processes in the world of business to commerce, and most goods are now decided, purchased, and delivery is arranged online. In the world of business-to-business and professional sales, this new technology is impacting across all functions in all enterprises but especially in the sales and marketing function. Automation and AI are replacing many marketing and sales roles but not all. The professional business-to-business salesperson will survive because that point in sales when there must be an exchange of high-value goods in a high-value transaction with multiple risk factors will always require human interaction. At this level, sales ability is basically a unique human skill that is instinctive but can be taught, practiced, and improved. Sales excellence at this level requires an understanding of what your prospective customer values the most. Becoming invaluable to your customer is the critical element in achieving sales excellence and is often referred to as consultative selling. This chapter focuses on explaining what that is, why it is important, and how to take advantage and prosper in sales and take advantage of the introduction of customer relationship management (CRM), automation, and AI.

Brief History of Sales

I have tried to summarize the last 100 years of the sales profession to illustrate how new technology has impacted every decade as shown in Figure 1.1. I have taken my inspiration from Roderick Jefferson in his recent book *Sales Enablement 3.0*[3] and have adapted, changed, and added to his version of the history of sales. As you can see, a professional approach to selling and training started with Dale Carnegie's book, which reflected a significant change in society at the time. Dale Carnegie became an instant success with the hugely popular *How to Win Friends and Influence People.*[4] Like most of his books, it revealed little that was

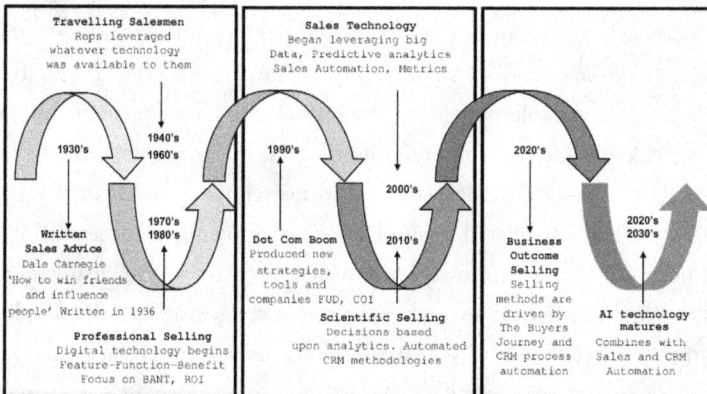

Figure 1.1 History of modern sales: 100 years of the sales profession

unknown about human psychology but stressed that an individual's attitude is crucial. His basic rules were don't criticize, condemn, or complain. Give honest and sincere appreciation. Arouse in the other person an eager want. Become genuinely interested in other people. You can still apply those rules successfully to selling and, in fact, to living successfully. He became a very successful American writer and lecturer, and the developer of courses in self-improvement, salesmanship, corporate training, public speaking, and interpersonal skills. Today, Dale Carnegie is a global organization with professional development courses in 35 languages across 80 countries. The company he started claims today that it has proven successful over 100 years and has made Dale Carnegie the industry leader in professional training and development.

The next evolution of selling driven by technology takes place in the 1970s and 1980s. Digital technology has started to influence society and selling. Mainframes from International Business Machines (IBM) dominated, and minicomputers from Digital Equipment Corporation were starting to make a huge impact. However, the biggest impact on the dominance of IBM and others was the arrival of the microcomputer or personal computer from fledgling companies like Apple Computer and Commodore in the early 1980s. For example, IBM did not believe that personal computers and desktop software were of significance, and in the late 1980s, it was weeks away from going bankrupt until Louis Gerstner Jr took over as CEO and changed everything. One big change was training became less intensive to save money. Gerstner describes what he had to do to force IBM to survive in his book, *Who Says Elephants Can't Dance?*[5] Up to the late 1980s, most companies trained their salespeople thoroughly before allowing them to start selling face-to-face with potential customers. For example, after formal training, all new IBM salespeople were not allowed to sell in the field until they had completed around a year shadowing a successful IBM salesperson.[6] The main message was how to explain to the customer the feature-function-benefit of each product or service being sold. Explanation worked as trust was created. The sellers were trained to focus on budget, authority, need, and timeline and return on investment.

Before putting a prospect into the pipeline, the salesperson had to establish whether the person they are building a relationship with has the authority, the budget, the need, and whether they have a time pressure. Finally, there had to be compelling proof that there was a good business case and return on their investment. All this data was entered into manual systems and if available, new software programs that recorded activity and represented the early CRM systems.

The technology matured, with personal computers becoming dominant, but the sales approach did not change much in the late 1980s to early 1990s, and selling evolved along the lines of the 1980s. Sales training became more sophisticated, and popular sales strategies, such as how to spread fear, uncertainty, and doubt in your prospects' mind and how to highlight the cost of investment (COI) and cost of ownership (COO), became dominant. Then, in the late 1990s, the new technology of the internet created the dot-com boom, which created a stock market bubble and just as quickly the early promise evaporated on Friday, March 10, 2000. The growth of the internet had created a buzz amongst investors, who were quick to pour money into startup companies. These companies were able to raise enough money to go public without a business plan, product, or track record of profits. These companies quickly ran through their cash, which caused them to go under.

Many people believe that the current buzz and promotion around AI may cause a similar bubble to be created and a similar crash to happen in the late 2020s. However, like the internet technology, which has matured and changed society, many also believe that AI will follow the same path and become the most significant technology ever created. The sales profession has a culture of the positive message of just do it, and often jumps on new technology and tries to apply new technology to their processes without generating the sales productivity that was expected from this huge financial investment. A good example is the modern 21st-century CRMs. They have created efficiencies but not effectiveness, with most research revealing that the win rate of professional sellers has stubbornly not changed or increased as expected. In early 2000, sales training had become an expensive luxury due to the dot-com crash and just-in-time global trade and commercial changes due to the emergence of the BRICS economies (Brazil, Russia, India, China, South Africa). Business and commerce were changing fast, and new priorities resulted in financial leaders being told that costs had to be reduced and money diverted to meet the rapid expansion of global trade driven by new internet technology. Sales training was one of the first budgets to be reduced or stopped completely. Sales process and methodology were replaced with CRM technology, and some took advantage of the new technology of hosting on the re-engineered internet technology, which was cheaper than salespeople on the road.

In 1999, four Salesforce founders, working shoulder to shoulder in a small San Francisco apartment, launched a CRM system with a groundbreaking twist. All the software and critical customer data would be hosted on the internet and made available as a subscription service. Salesforce Inc. is now a hugely successful cloud-based software company headquartered in San Francisco, California. It provides CRM software and applications focused on sales, customer service, marketing automation, e-commerce, analytics, and application development. The next stage for the company is building AI platforms and agents to be integrated in all its technology. More about that later.

By the early 2010s, the massive impact of the new cloud and internet technology created a significant move to applying scientific analysis to decision making and therefore to selling. The early analytics programs started in the 1970s and were initially applied in the sports industry but had now matured and moved into business processes. For example, SPSS Statistics, which was a statistical software suite developed for data management, advanced analytics, multivariate analysis, business intelligence (BI), and criminal investigation, was acquired by IBM in 2009. In addition, the impact of the iPhone, launched in 2008, destroyed the Blackberry phone success overnight and then combined with email and other digital and internet global technologies to create the social media revolution. In his book on Steve Jobs,[7] Walter Isaacson describes how the Apple iPhone and Steve Jobs changed society forever and, of course, had a huge impact on the sales profession.

By the 2020s, this new digital technological revolution combined with the new CRM and AI technologies has resulted in sales methodology and processes increasingly becoming automated. It is estimated by the Rain Group, in their publication on virtual selling,[8] that 80 percent of all current sales professionals will no longer exist by 2030. Their evidence and reasoning points to the commercial development that only high-value products and services will require face-to-face or virtual interaction in the future. Everything else will be a commodity, which will be investigated, proven, and purchased via the internet and online. Assuming this forecast is correct, then it is critical the sales professionals of today understand that to be successful, now and in the future, their selling journey and selling methods must be aligned with their customers' decision makers and stakeholders' buying journey. The ability and skills required to achieve this objective are contained in the Sales Excellence Framework explained in this book.

How Has Sales Changed Today?

To summarize, the old role of sales was to show customers why your product and services are better than those of your competitor. This approach is no longer viable and has a high failure rate. It is also too expensive, and customers do not want walking, talking brochures. In their book *Virtual Selling,* Mike Schultz, Dave Shaby, and Andy Springer's research revealed that the new modern successful salesperson is a highly skilled value creator. They position their pitch around business outcomes instead of technology. They differentiate themselves by creatively helping to solve customer problems with key insights. They are measured by customers against the value they create. To create value, they must fully understand the issues and concerns of their customers' senior management/directors and C-level executives (CEO, CFO, COO, CIO, and CRO).

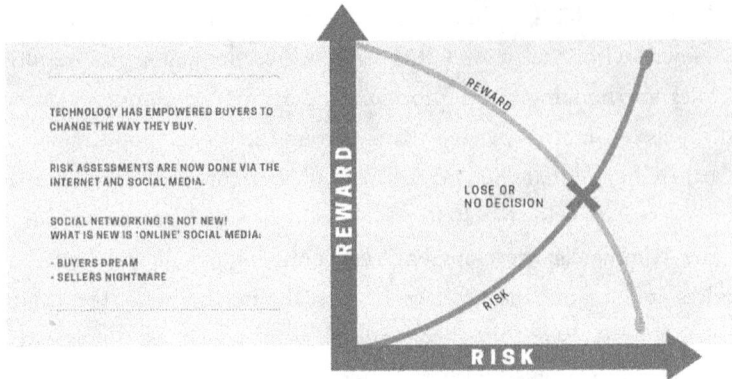

TECHNOLOGY HAS EMPOWERED BUYERS TO
CHANGE THE WAY THEY BUY.

RISK ASSESSMENTS ARE NOW DONE VIA THE
INTERNET AND SOCIAL MEDIA.

SOCIAL NETWORKING IS NOT NEW!
WHAT IS NEW IS 'ONLINE' SOCIAL MEDIA:

- BUYERS DREAM
- SELLERS NIGHTMARE

REWARD

RISK

REWARD

LOSE OR
NO DECISION

RISK

Figure 1.2 Risk versus reward

What Has Not Changed?

Mike Weinberg, a multipublished author and well-regarded sales coach, states in his book *New Sales Simplified*[9] that prospective customers are not interested in what you do, they are only interested in what you can do for them. Every human being is interested in WIFMs, which means what's in it for me. The process of buying and selling is dictated by human interaction. Humans are averse to any risk but crave new things and desire rewards. We all like to buy things!

But when risk overtakes reward, we will not buy. Figure 1.2 illustrates this simple fact. High-performing salespeople understand this fact. In complex, high-value consultative selling when risk becomes higher than reward, then the sale will slip or fail completely, and the customer will go for the safe option. It is the role of the salesperson today to always mitigate risk and emphasize the specific value they personally bring combined with the reward of their product or service.[10]

The prospective customer, on the other hand, is only interested in removing any blocks to their strategic business outcomes, company and personal goals, key performance indicators, and bonuses. Any business problem or issue that blocks these goals must be removed, and the illustrated buying process is therefore initiated. Figure 1.3 shows the buyer cycle from first being aware of a company issue or problem that they need to assess and measure the impact on the business to measur-

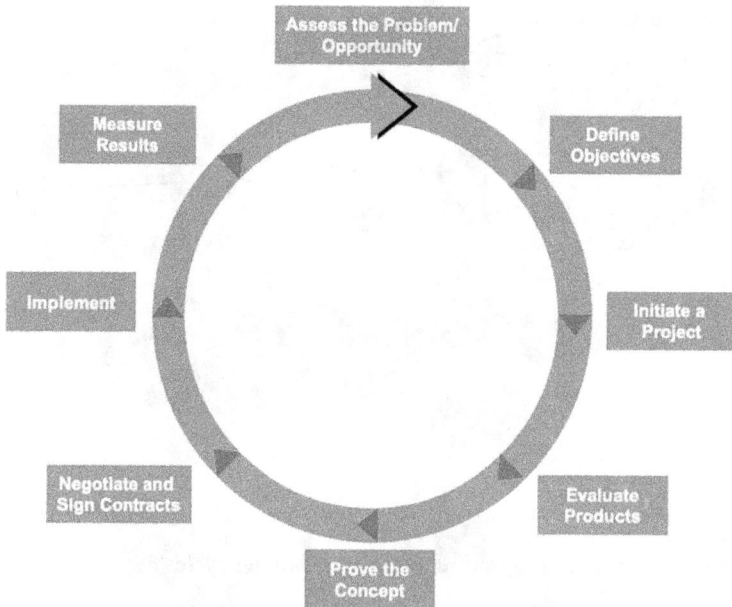

Figure 1.3 The buying cycle

ing the results after their successful or not-so-successful implemented solution.

Increasingly, buyers in the business-to-business environments are using online services to make decisions and then source products and even sometimes install products and services downloaded from websites. The results can be disastrous, as seen in the recent example in Britain of the TSB IT crash of December 20, 2022, when investigators concluded that widespread and serious failings in planning software updates resulted in significant disruption to customers. It transpired that a critical piece of software had not been tested after being downloaded and installed.

The sales cycle must follow the buyer cycle as shown in Figure 1.4 to achieve sales excellence. There are four types of sellers in most sales teams. These types of sellers are aligned in the graphic with the buyer cycle stages to show the effectiveness of each type at each stage. They are the sales excellence sellers, the problem solver seller, the credible source seller, and the supplier seller. For example, you can see that although the supplier seller needs a very short sales cycle they must find a huge

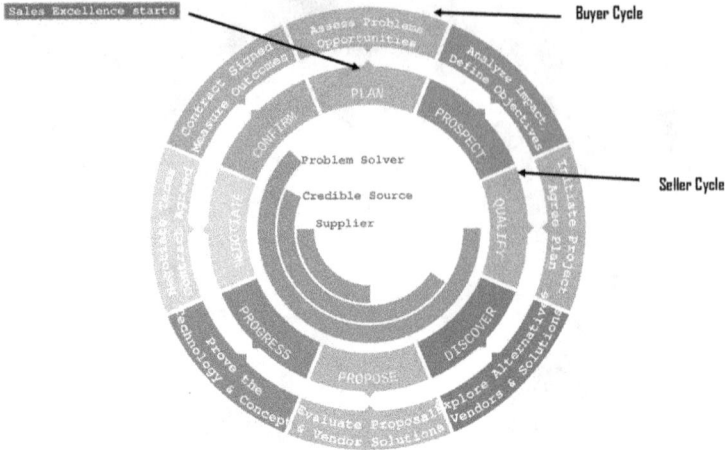

Sales Excellence:
This requires the ability to be with the Buyer from Assess Problems to Measure Outcomes.

Figure 1.4 Combining selling cycle with buying cycle

number of low-value opportunities to reach their target, and their win rate is very low. The sales excellence seller, on the other hand, needs a smaller number of higher value opportunities, has a longer sales cycle, builds a higher-quality pipeline, and has a very high win rate.

Research highlighted in the book *The Challenger Sale* by Matt Dixon and Brent Adamson[11] concluded that todays' buyer goes much further into the buying process without the seller. They also concluded that classic relationship building is a losing approach, especially when it comes to selling complex, large-scale business-to-business solutions. The authors' study found that every salesperson in the world falls into one of five distinct profiles, and while all these types can deliver average sales performance, only one, the challenger, delivers consistently high performance. Not all research supports their conclusions, but the publication made many sales leaders rethink their sale approaches.

Instead of bludgeoning customers with endless facts and features about their company and products, the challenger approach to customers is to lead with unique insights about how customers can save or make money. They tailor their sales message to the customer's specific needs and objectives. Rather than acquiescing to the customer's every demand or objection, they are assertive, pushing back when necessary and taking control of the sale.

I agree with some of their conclusions, especially the ability to have unique business insights, which is critical for success, but I prefer to simplify the definition of a successful seller in today's world. In my experience, 80 percent of sellers are made up of three types. The first category is genuine "problem solvers," who are often on or close to their sales targets. Managers spend much of their scarce time trying to help them close their deals. The second type is sellers who can be described as a "credible source" and often are just below target and managers often say "could do better." Managers find this type very frustrating, and their forecasts are often too optimistic. Third, there are sellers who operate as merely vendors/suppliers who focus on quickly supplying whatever the customer asks to be demonstrated. These sellers last for perhaps one/two years and then move on once they have drained all the easy opportunities created by marketing or existing customers. The win percentages of the above three types of sellers range from 25 percent, where their win ratio is 1:4, to as low as 10 percent, where their win rate is 1:10, and their sales forecasts are always wrong, with regular slipped deals every quarter.

The fourth type of seller demonstrates "sales excellence." They go beyond CRM and sales automation capabilities. Their win rate is at least 1:2, and their sales forecasts are always accurate. They are always the top 20 percent who can be relied upon to consistently achieve sales excellence and are always on or above their sales targets. Most sales managers and sales directors depend on these excellors to ensure they hit their own targets. C-level executives in sales organizations often stay close to these sellers and can believe and trust their sales forecasts.

Recent buyer research in the book *Insight Selling* by Mike Schultz and John E. Doerr highlights the dramatic change in buyer behavior and states that many sellers and sales organizations are out of step with buyer organizations[12]. Top performers know this and have already changed their approach and doubled down on learning new sales skills and improving their existing skillset. The top five skills quoted by customers that they value in salespeople are they educated me with new ideas or perspectives, they collaborated with me, they persuaded me we would achieve our desired results, they listened to me, they understood my needs.

Sales excellence requires all five skillsets. You need to understand and always be aligned with your buyer journey and his business in their buying process. For example, if you are first introduced to a prospective customer only by their request for a quote then you are late to the buying process. You must quickly work out how to be of real value to your customer or prospect. You must create sales goals and sales activities linked to your typical CRM that also align with your buyer's journey, goals, and activities. Critically, your sales process must align with or follow the buyer's journey regardless of where the first contact begins. This means in the example you must go backward in your sales approach. You are not ready to provide a quote. You do not know or understand their business. If you do send a quote then you are already at a disadvantage and you will not be able to create or provide unique value.

There is a basic principle and simple truth in the goal of achieving sales excellence. The most important principle is you must align your activities with those of your buyers and stakeholders. This principle of alignment if not followed by the sales management will result in a huge gulf and mismatch between strategy and field execution and will nullify any of the latest new technology being implemented and applied, especially AI. This fact is highlighted by Frank Cespedes research in his book *Aligning Strategy and Sales*.[12-13] To be able to excel at selling today, you must be able to apply new technology, but for that to be effective, you must align your activities with your buyer, which means that you must know the customer's business plan, revealing the prospective customers business problems, issues, and cost of these issues almost before the customer themselves is aware of the impact. Each chapter in this book provides a practical method of taking the customer and the buyers at each stage to the door of your solution, opening the door to reveal it, and walking with them through the door as a trusted advisor to help them adopt it.

What Is the Impact of Sales Automation Technology and AI on Sales?

In sales teams, the usual picture is that the top 10 to 20 percent often contribute up to 80 percent of the profitable sales revenue.[14] The rest of the sales team is usually under target and can deliver as low as 20 percent of the profitable sale revenue. This is an expensive business model, and many C-level executives are asking themselves why they are paying such huge salaries to the sales division. There must be another way. So the current hot topic to save money and expense is sales automation like Salesforce.com, SugarCRM, AI embedded in CRMs, and now standalone AI applications and solutions like Gong, Gemini, and so on.

The data produced from your sales goals and activities feed into your CRM, sales automation, and AI systems and must accurately inform these systems. Remember GIGO which means if you put garbage in then you get garbage out. In addition, incorrect data will distort your AI and sales automation software outcomes. As a result, you will be led down a path that will seem exciting and will increasingly give you confidence that all is well, but it is a false path. You will spend a great deal of time educating your prospective customer, which will only help your competition. You will then probably lose the sale or, at the very least, the sale will slip to the next quarter or later. If your pipeline is poor, then you will probably become desperate and push the buyer who will invariably ask for a large discount and improbable terms and conditions that you may well not be able to meet in the implementation phase, if you eventually close the sale. However, this sale will cost you much more in time and money than expected and planned. Ultimately, your reputation will be harmed, and company branded as poor.

A recent survey in 2024 by the CRM company SugarCRM revealed that almost 60 percent of the respondents reported that CRM is more important for achieving sales and marketing goals compared to five years ago. That's a powerful statement on CRM's evolution. The report also discovered that 45 percent (also the top response) say the top priority for maximizing value from CRM will be gaining a complete view of all customer interactions. The report points out the importance of working from a single source of truth where every stakeholder has a clear view of all customer-facing activities. This, they claim, will help sales teams craft the most relevant engagement to move customers down their journey with the chosen branded product.

But this single source of truth must achieve accurate data input from the salespeople, marketing, and other functions who input data.

The top areas customers reported most impacted by an effective CRM are forecasting and pipeline visibility, quality and quantity of leads, analytics, and AI. When asked about the most important areas of sales and marketing that CRM has helped optimize, the top three answers were pipeline visibility (37 percent), quality of leads (35 percent), and quantity of leads (31 percent). One of the key conclusions is that CRM is increasingly used as an intelligent tool to accurately predict future sales activity and gain key insights on prospects and existing customers. This is being achieved because companies no longer need to rely on separate BI tools to talk to their CRM. Now AI and BI tools are all embedded in most CRM platforms, with analytical capabilities available at sales organizations' fingertips without having to enlist the services of a data scientist.

Case Study 1: A Cautionary Tale About Using AI Tools in the Sales Process

Many salespeople today are being introduced to AI tools embedded in their CRM or used as standalone tools. AI tools are best used to support your sales approach but not replace it. In this real-world example, an experienced seller describes how he uses Gong. What it does well and what it does not do well.

The following is a direct quote from a seller using the AI application "Gong" actively in today's buyer's marketplace.

I've used Gong to help me record my discovery calls when I'm speaking to Prospects. The tool has helped me to concentrate on the prospect when asking questions, which is great, But unfortunately the product didn't help me move forward or provide me feedback on the next steps or questions I could have asked, nor does it provide structure. By contrast Toms sales tools helped me by providing dynamically interactive structure to my calls and context. It's really allowed me to engage with the prospect's deeper buying motivations and ask more in depth questions. Having Tom's tools allows me to understand the clear next steps and provides useful methods to unlock a clear return on investment (ROI) for my customer. It's really helped me not only progress deals but to close out pipeline.

In this example, the seller is using an AI tool called Gong to help him perform what the sales profession calls discovery. This stage is critical, and I cover it in detail in Chapter 6. Good discovery questions should start with a unique insight from the seller to the buyer and then continue to reveal and create new business insights. AI tools are very good at determining the best questions to ask at first, but there is a problem that is highlighted by the seller's comments above and is a recognized issue with AI today. Human beings are not logical. AI programming is based on utilizing and copying how human being neural networks work in the brain. However, a customer will often reply to a discovery question with either a vague or indeed a deliberately false answer to test the seller's sincerity and knowledge. AI tools learn quickly but their programming is geared to giving an answer to a question which is the best or most likely probability answer based on AI's capability to access patterns in huge databases of knowledge. An irrational question and answer process produces an error-prone question and answer result from an AI tool. This issue for example is causing problems in automatic online and phone-based customer support AI tools. A customer online or on the phone can be irrational in their answers to specific questions. The AI tool responds in a confused way and leaves the customer frustrated who then signs off from the website, losing the customer sale or interest. That is what the seller above referred to as not providing feedback nor the next questions to ask. AI cannot replicate or deal with irrational thought nor can it provide insightful decisions because it is a support methodology, not a decision-based methodology.

Case Study 2: Global Construction Company and AI

(This real-world example is linked to the same case study example in Chapter 11.)

To re-emphasize the advantages but also the severe limitations of AI in the interactive dynamic sales process this is an example I used in Chapter 11 of a global construction company sales opportunity. Like many potential customers today, they had progressed quite a bit into their buying process before contacting the sales organization. As research has shown most buyers are 70 percent into the buying process before contacting their chosen sales organization. In this case, that fact is critical to the ultimate success or failure of the seller being able to win the sale.

This is a real example that I coached recently, but we cannot use the actual names due to their still live nondisclosure agreement. The sales organization, we shall call Lightning Software, was approached by this Global Construction Company with specific requests for their Global HR and payroll divisions. It was a potential multimillion-dollar deal.

The Lightning Software sales organization uses Gemini and other AI tools to help guide their sellers. The senior salesperson in this example asked Gemini "Give me advice on the best Strategy our company Lightning Software should use to win this sale with this Global Construction Company XYZ."

The following text in italics is the exact written response from Gemini. It is good general sales process advice; it is comprehensive and could genuinely act as an accurate guide for most inexperienced salespeople and most customer situations. However, you will quickly see how this advice is in fact nonspecific, too general, and not interactive. In addition, when the seller actively engages with the customer stakeholders, it becomes evident very quickly that the customer wants to start the process at the proof of concept and negotiation stage. They believe they know what they want and want to negotiate a price and have a demonstration with their live data. Consequently, the seller asks Gemini after each customer visit for more advice. The AI responses become increasingly irrelevant to the real situation, and the sale starts to slip and is in danger of being lost altogether. I am called in as a sales coach to the sales team and we apply the interactive, dynamic sales coaching tools contained in this book. We apply the abilities and required skills to successfully interact and engage with multiple stakeholders who are often vague and offer incomplete descriptions of their very specific business needs. AI remains a supportive guide but does not and should never become the decision maker in the process of determining critical actions and steps to achieve the purchase order.

As is demonstrated in Chapter 11, the key to ultimate success in this deal was for the seller to understand how to align their sales process with the construction company's complex buyer process and decide what actions to take that would win the sale. In other words, AI knows **what** to do generally but we need to be constantly focusing on specifically **how** to achieve the sale and **why** we are deciding the actions. AI tools cannot do this task. However, as you can see below, AI provides a very good description of what the required basic sales process is for any sale in any industry with solutions on offer. That is valuable, but not the essential ingredient for success.

What Follows Is the Exact Written Text Response to the Question From Gemini AI

Consulting Advice for Lightning Software's Sales Strategy with the Global Construction Company XYZ.

Understanding the Client's Needs.   The key to winning this multimillion dollar deal lies in thoroughly understanding the construction company's specific needs and demonstrating Lightning Software's unique value proposition. Here's a breakdown:

1. *Integration Complexity: Their 200 subsidiaries and 200 existing software programs highlight their critical need for seamless integration.*
2. *Reduced Competition: While IBM might be present, focus on Lightning Software's specific strengths, not just competition.*

Lightning Software's Winning Arguments.

1. *Integration Expertise: Emphasize Lightning Software's proven track record in integrating complex HR and ERP systems (Enterprise Resource Systems) across large enterprises. Showcase successful case studies with similar challenges.*
2. *Reduced Total Cost of Ownership (TCO): Highlight how Lightning Software's solution can streamline operations, eliminate redundancy, and potentially save the construction company money in the long run.*
3. *Industry-Specific Knowledge: Demonstrate an understanding of the unique challenges faced by the construction industry in terms of HR and ERP management.*
4. *Scalability and Flexibility: Lightning Software's solution should cater to the company's global reach and diverse needs across 200 subsidiaries.*
5. *Implementation and Onboarding: Outline a clear and efficient plan for implementation, data migration, and user onboarding across all subsidiaries.*

Framing a Win–Win Scenario.

1. *Focus on Business Outcomes: Don't just sell software, sell the improved efficiency, cost savings, and streamlined operations Lightning Software's solution can deliver.*
2. *Reduced Risk: Position Lightning Software as the lower-risk option due to its expertise in handling complex integrations.*
3. *Long-Term Partnership: Express Lightning Software's commitment to a long-term partnership, providing ongoing support and adapting to the construction company's evolving needs.*

Consultative Sales Approach.

1. *Discovery Sessions: Conduct in-depth discovery sessions to understand the construction company's specific pain points and desired outcomes.*

2. *Collaborative Solution Design: Work collaboratively with the client's IT and HR teams to create a customized solution that seamlessly integrates with their existing systems.*
3. *Transparent Communication: Maintain open and transparent communication throughout the sales process, addressing concerns proactively.*

Additional Considerations.

1. *Proof of Concept (POC): If possible, propose a Proof of Concept showcasing how Lightning Software's solution can integrate specific systems within a limited scope.*
2. *Executive Sponsorship: Cultivate relationships with key decision makers at the construction company, including C-suite executives.*
3. *Value Quantification: Present a clear and measurable value proposition that quantifies the potential cost savings and return on investment (ROI) from using Lightning Software's solution.*

Remember, Lightning Software doesn't just compete on price, they compete on value. By demonstrating a deep understanding of the client's challenges, superior integration capabilities, and a commitment to long-term success, Lightning Software can secure this multimillion dollar deal.

Bonus Tip: While Lightning Software.com provides general information, consider creating a targeted landing page specifically addressing the challenges of large construction companies with complex HR and ERP needs. This focused page can serve as a valuable resource for the construction company during their evaluation process.

It is important to understand that AI and machine learning models are based on principles and equations taken from physics that have been interpreted and used by computer programmers to create AI software tools in the IT industry and others. The 2024 Nobel Prize in Physics was awarded to John J. Hopfield and Geoffrey E. Hinton for "foundational discoveries and inventions that enable machine learning with artificial neural networks" (www.nobelprize.org/prizes/physics/).[15] John Hopfield created an associative memory that can store and reconstruct images and other types of patterns in data. Geoffrey Hinton invented a method that can autonomously find properties in data, and so perform tasks such as identifying specific elements in pictures. On winning this prize, the physics laureates were quoted as saying "our main concern and worry with AI future development is that AI is used to replace human beings' decision making rather than act as a critical decision support tool to help human endeavour succeed" (BBC radio October 4, 2024).

Therefore, in the previous case study example 1, due to his lack of good discovery skills the seller wanted Gong to do the discovery process for him and help him understand the customer's feedback and provide new innovative business insights. AI will attempt this process if asked, but it will do it badly because there is no logical pattern that AI can interpret at this stage in the sales process. AI-enabled sales software will help in suggesting good discovery questions, but deciding how to then delve deeper into those customers' answers to discover their ultimate motivation and reasons to buy is a distinctly human and irrational process without obvious recognizable patterns.

In case study example 2, the global construction company has already progressed to negotiating and proving their chosen software and they know what they want. In both cases, the business insight skill provided in the self-coaching sales skills described in this book is essential to success and is what the high-performing, high-value, successful salespeople must possess to be successful in today's business world (see also Chapter 6).

Sales teams that can quickly evaluate opportunities based on accurate data from CRMs and AI tools are better positioned to maintain a healthy pipeline. However, to repeat a key fact, the purpose of data and knowledge is to inform and support decision making, but that data must be accurate. In addition, you need to know how to use and apply that data and knowledge to execute the sales process correctly. Sales leaders who invest in combining these essential advanced sales skills with AI tools will create and develop high-performing sales teams. The next eight chapters will directly show you how to achieve this goal. But first, you need to know how people learn new skills.

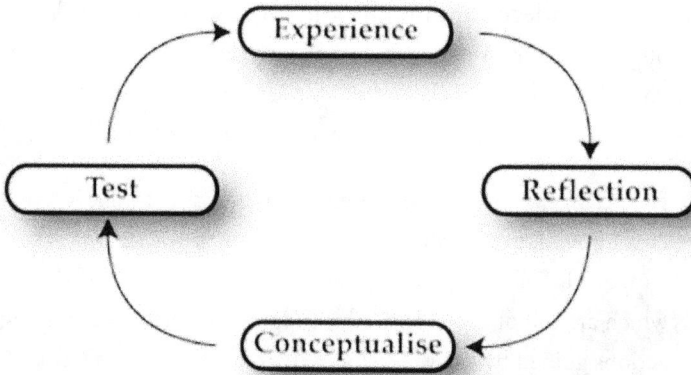

Figure 1.5 The four stages of learning

Why the Theory and Practice of Learning Is Important to Achieve Sales Excellence

In the business of sales, consistent success is only achieved by refreshing existing skills, learning new skills, practicing the application of skills, and planning before action. Knowing what and why you are doing something is important. Knowing how to do it is critical.

Attending a one-off sales training course is not enough. All research into training of any kind reveals that attendees forget 80 percent of what they have been taught within three days, unless it is constantly reinforced over the next nine months and again two to three years later. To learn and embed new or improved skills into your daily processes, you must first act, reflect what worked and what did not, repeat action, reflect on again, learn and apply a new revised action, and then repeat the process until it sticks and changes behavior.[16]

The next section takes a quick look at how people learn, why it is important to know, and how the theory and practice of learning is integrated and embedded into the Sales Excellence Framework to help you acquire, learn, and improve sales excellence skills.

The most important conclusion on all the recent research on how people learn is the statement from Professor Eric Mazur, physicist, and educator from Harvard University who simply concluded we learn more by doing.[17] What he meant by that statement is that once we acquire the necessary knowledge, then learning how to use that knowledge and embedding it in our everyday behavior and working life requires a process that David A. Kolb, the father of all experiential learning theory, illustrated as in Figure 1.5, which is my interpretation of his theory.

1. **Experience.** A concrete experience of a new situation is encountered, or a reinterpretation of existing experience. What happened? Sellers usually put those results into their CRM, which are full of errors and value judgments. They keep redoing actions guided by their CRM and their AI tools until success is achieved or until they move on to the next opportunity. No learning or change in behaviors takes place. There is no circle of learning, but a continuous circle of let's keep doing the same thing until I get the result I want. Some people describe that approach as madness.

2. **Reflection.** Observation of the new experience takes place. Of particular importance are any inconsistencies between action and actual experience to then create real understanding. Most sellers don't have the time for this, nor the framework to reflect on what went well, what did not and how can they change.

3. **Conceptualize.** The process of reflection gives rise to a new idea or a modification of an existing abstract concept. Sellers should ask, what will I do differently? Sales managers should become the coach at this stage but are busy with 80 percent of their time spent on reports and CRM statistics. Sellers need to make a new concrete action and approach, but many sellers have already committed actions in their CRM and so carry the same actions but keep trying harder.

4. **Test.** Active experimentation needs to be achieved by the seller who must apply a different action to the customer world around them to see what results are gained and then restart their learning/sales process again. This is when real learning occurs, and consequently, behavior change happens when this new approach starts to work and brings the desired results.

However, many sales managers say this learning process is not possible in the field and so sales automation and CRM are increasingly followed by the manager and seller as an easy and quick fix. Training is reduced and automation increased. Sales productivity and effectiveness are then reduced, but activity and reporting efficiency are increased, which provide the managers with false reassurance and a sense that all is well. Recent research reveals that increasingly senior executives of companies who have invested millions in CRM systems are unhappy because this investment has not generated the expected increase in sales revenue and productivity.

What Figure 1.5 highlights is that effective learning and behavior change do not happen just by doing something. Learning and behavior change only occurs when a seller can execute all four stages of the model. In addition, the most important action that sellers can do to learn is to reflect on their actions. Reflection can be summarized as follows.

Ask yourself these questions and write down the answers:

- What did I set out to achieve?
- What did I do?
- What went well and, what might I do differently in the future?
- What worked and what didn't work as I intended?
- What evidence do I have to support my view of what worked and what didn't work?
- What does the sales training literature say about how I could approach the sales session differently to make it more effective?
- If my approach worked, how could it work better?

You will notice in the next chapters that these questions are embedded in the Sales Excellence Framework checklist, techniques, and tools. Each chapter describes how the critical sales skillsets are applied to gain and sustain your desired sales results.

In summary, most sellers are doers. They get it done. They pitch for business, and if that experience is successful they carry on doing. Even if unsuccessful they often still carry on doing the same thing, moving from customer to customer until they get their desired sales result.

They make their sales target and so that reinforces the belief that this approach is correct. But just doing is not enough for long-term success and learning. The just-do-it approach is very wasteful of resources and time and is inconsistent, unpredictable, and unreliable, as any good but frustrated sales manager will tell you. It does not work. The key to gaining excellence is to understand how to learn and change your behavior. So, after doing, then stop, reflect, redo, and rethink and do again. The next chapters describe how you can learn to do this and achieve the sales success you deserve.

CHAPTER 2

Creating the Ingredients

Identifying the Eight Basic "Hard" Sales Skills to Gain Sales Excellence

You need to be developing techniques, activities, and checklists linked to your CRM (Customer Relationship Manager), AI, and sales automation systems to build the sales skills that produce sales excellence.

This chapter focuses on the critical factor of identifying and learning **how** to achieve the essential skills to achieve sales excellence.

In my experience, sales excellence today can be summarized in the following process, which I have seen applied by the top-performing sellers:

- GRAB Customer Prospect Attention by showing INSIGHT to key Business Problems
- IDENTIFY Problems that BLOCK their key STRATEGIC BUSINESS OBJECTIVES
- QUANTIFY IMPACT of the BUSINESS PAINS caused by Business Problems
- SEPARATE their TECHNICAL PAINS and LINK each to specific BUSINESS PAINS
- HIGHLIGHT YOUR UNIQUE CAPABILITY to solve TECHNICAL PAINS to then remove linked BUSINESS PAINS and so achieve BUSINESS OUTCOMES and OBJECTIVES
- NOW PROVE IT with YOUR UNIQUE SOLUTION
- CUSTOMER UNIQUE VALUE is achieved

However, to achieve the aforementioned process successfully, the salesperson must gain the abilities and skills to achieve a sale in what is a complex, difficult, and frustratingly hard-to-apply interactive nonsequential process. These are known as 'hard' sales skill sets and are detailed in Figure 2.1 together with a sales excellence checklist and a set of techniques and tools to improve sales performance. To sustain sales excellence over time, the high-performing salespeople always work on improving their skills. The tried-and-tested techniques and tools in this book, when applied correctly, will help you to reach sales excellence and achieve repeatable and predictable sales revenue results. However, like all top performers, you need to be constantly learning and applying the remedial tools that will help all sellers reach their full potential. A key ingredient to learning how to achieve sales excellence is identifying, understanding, and improving the eight "hard" skills of selling. The hard skills suggested are based on respected buyer/seller research plus four decades of practice. Don't make assumptions about anything during your sales process and reduce your expectations to a minimum.

Apply the checklist for excellence questions in Figure 2.1. If you can honestly answer yes to all the questions and are also currently on target, then move on to Chapter 12 and start applying the self-coaching sales excellence framework. If you have doubts and feel you may need help in

The 'Hard Skillsets'	Checklist for Excellence	Techniques and Tools
Business Planning	Have I completed my Plan?	Account Research, Growth Plan, Executive Checklist, Prioritize Accounts
Business Development	Have I found my Hot Prospects?	Development Circle, Sales call Story, Activity Schedule, Pipeline Growth
Opportunity Identification	Is my Deal Real?	Qualify In/Out, Validate Opportunity, Score Opportunity, Metrics Tool
Business Insight	Delivered Business Insights?	Business Insights, Influence Map, Directional Questions, Insights Tool
Solution Proposal	Client Value in Client Terms?	Checklist, Presentation Planning, Proposal Template, Solution Tool
Proving and Progressing	Is my Solution Compelling?	Deal Reviews, Team Selling, Progress Actions, Progress Scorecard Tool
Negotiation and Agreement	From a Position of Strength?	Call Plan, Objection Skills, Negotiation Sheet, Give/Get Terms Tool
Confirmation and Implementation	Will I gain at least 3 Referrals?	Confirm Value, Implementation, Referrals Sheet, Post Sales Checklist Tool

Figure 2.1 Identifying and improving the eight "hard sales skills"

certain sales skills, then carry on reading. To help you improve any of the skills in Figure 2.1, then you need specialized techniques and tools to improve, gain, and sustain sales excellence.

The eight sales skill sets and the desired outcomes.

1. Business planning: Prioritized key accounts, researched accounts, be on quota
2. Business development: Prospected for new business and grow pipeline
3. Opportunity identification: Qualified and quantified opportunity with metrics
4. Business insight: Discovered insights and identify key stakeholders
5. Business outcomes: Proposed solution and proven return on investment
6. Proof and progress: Progressed and linked technical capability to business
7. Negotiation and agreement: Negotiated the "need," give to get and get to the Purchase Order.
8. Implementation and delivery: Confirm customer value received, driven teamwork

The above skill sets can be divided into four key interconnected and interactive approaches.

1. Business planning and business development.
2. Opportunity identification and business insight.
3. Progress and negotiate.
4. Implement and confirm

Business Planning and Business Development

The first two skill sets require interconnected techniques and tools of planning and prospecting. These are two critical and interconnected activities that are often the last thing done in the day-to-day activities of salespeople and their sales managers. Creating a plan is usually done at the request of your sales manager at the beginning of the year, then forgotten about once presented to your boss. Prospecting activity often proves the statement: the road to failure is paved with good intentions. In other words, most salespeople are full of good intentions and want to prospect every day, but many become distracted by daily demands on their time. More often, salespeople get excited and distracted by hot leads dropping into their CRM from marketing or presales. For example, sellers rush to complete a high-value request for pricing (RFP) from a large but previously unknown potential customer, but without any attempt to apply the discipline of qualifying and discovering the business issues to determine whether this opportunity is winnable and worth committing scarce company resources. The result is lost or slipped forecasted sales six months later. The following linked planning and prospecting and planning techniques, combined with the tools in Chapter 4, will ensure these activities are completed enthusiastically because they generate predictable sales results.

To repeat, many salespeople will naturally jump to and be excited by the latest hot lead or request for RFPs from a key account or large customer. It may seem counterintuitive, but the last thing salespeople or managers should do is react to an apparently hot opportunity. All sales research evidence demonstrates that if you are not first in to create and help the customer identify and solve a business problem, then your chances of success are reduced considerably. If the prospective customer contacts you first, before you do, then you are already too late in the buying process. Planning what, why, and who to sell to and then combining that with a quality, well-researched account prospecting schedule are always the first essential activities that must be done and must be updated every day. This is the key step to gaining and achieving sales excellence.

Evidence from sales research consistently identify the reason for poor sales, slipped sales, or less than expected sales revenue. The sales manager and sellers did not have a plan that they followed, could not easily amend an existing plan, could not react proactively to significant changes in customers' needs and demands, and were prospecting the wrong potential customers.

The consequence of not having a flexible realistic plan and linked prospecting schedule is poor-quality pipeline and lack of real winnable sales opportunities, and so the sellers are always under target and will be under pressure.

According to Blount, in his book *Fanatical Prospecting*,[1] he describes looking for new business as the lifeblood of any company' success and depends on building a high-performing sales team. However, it is probably the least favorite activity of all salespeople. So much so that a multitude of agencies and services have sprung up to satisfy the demand and need of salespeople. However, if this approach becomes the only method to gain hot leads, then they can make sellers lazy, and increasingly they will rely solely on these services for leads. The leads can increase in number from these agencies but often become poor quality. Sales excellence and high performance deteriorate, and effective sales techniques and tools are needed even more than before because the services and systems create a dependency by the seller on relying on systems creating new business leads. The result is the key "hard" skills of planning and gaining new business start to wither on the vine as the saying goes due to the lack of use and poor application. Revenue decreases and good sellers can become frustrated and often leave the company. The evidence shows that a combined approach of good systems plus constant refreshing and learning the "hard" sales skills is best and increases revenue.

Opportunity Identification and Business Insight

The three most common reasons why forecasted sales slip or are lost completely are, first, the financial impact of the business problem presented by the prospective customer is unknown and has not been identified and quantified, so there is no real sales opportunity. Second, there is no real business insight or understanding of the potential customers business nor is there deep knowledge of the personal and company-desired business outcomes of the key stakeholders. Third, action is not linked to removing real blocks that stop executives from achieving their strategic business objectives, so there is no real value to them or their company in purchasing the offered solution.

Progress and Negotiate

The most common reasons why any sales organization will bring in an experienced sales coach or sales training and enablement company is they have discovered that the biggest issue is sales revenue forecasts are often not accurate and never met. In addition, sales managers and executives are regularly surprised that good-quality and potentially high-value deals are being unexpectedly lost or slip regularly every quarter to the next quarter or even the next year..

Implement and Confirm

The biggest cause of salespeople and sales organizations getting a bad name and poor reputation is as soon as the order is taken they disappear from the customer relationship to be replaced by administration, technical, and implementation teams. All research reveals that customers hate this, and their view of success is almost opposite to the sales organizations view. Amazingly, this handover approach continues to be dominant in most companies. Smarter sales organizations have realized that the best place to gain referrals and new business opportunities is from happy existing customers. To this end, the sellers continue to be paid to be involved and to supervise, or in some cases lead, the technical and implementation teams. In effect, they become part of the customers' team. The result is that those sellers gain repeat business and inside knowledge as trusted advisers and gain hot leads and referrals to other similar companies in their marketplace and industry. People still buy from trusted people and sources.

Company executives and sales managers common reaction to poor forecasting, slipped deals, and low-performing sales teams is to invest heavily in lead-generation CRM and sales automation, and now AI. They split their resources, sales process, and sales teams into separate functions and personnel.

The results after these significant financial investments over the last 10 years have been very disappointing, which all recent research has confirmed and demonstrated. Sales revenue results and win rates are not increasing, especially in the business-to-business sectors. For example, a company I recently coached had invested heavily in the most popular CRM, sales automation programs, and AI apps. This was followed by the executives completely changing the structure of the sales organisation with a split of sales activities into 5 groups; pre-sales development teams, internal sales teams, external sales teams, key account managers, and new business sales teams. While this approach seemed eminently sensible and is becoming very popular, especially with presales increasingly using AI and sales automation, the sales message and marketing messages from the company were now not aligned, followed, nor presented uniformly to their prospective customers. This caused confusion and a mixed message to all customers. As a result, I was called in to coach the team of 75 salespeople divided into five teams with the goal of achieving better results. I applied the tools and techniques contained in this book and results improved immediately. So much so that the group sales director used the opportunity metric tool as a bolt-on extra to his CRM systems. Preparing a proposal was very costly at thousands of pounds, and so it was agreed that no proposal would be invested in unless it passed the opportunity metrics. This not only saved significant money, but there was also a significant increase in the number of winning proposals.

Another example is a sales director, whose team I had coached in his previous role, discovering that the monthly review and weekly cadences by his sales managers, which he had inherited, were ad hoc and had no structure. He quickly added the progress scorecard as another bolt-on extra to his cadence and review systems, and over six months, improved his win rate from winning 1:6 deals to 1:3 deals.

Therefore, what follows has been the result of deep research and multiple coaching sessions with a proven set of tools and techniques that, when applied correctly, address and solve the most common sales management issues by providing a methodology that guides the sellers, while at the same time ensuring everyone is talking from the same page and following the company's agreed marketing message.

CHAPTER 3

Business Planning

How to Gain Effective Business Plans

In Chapter 2, we identified the eight "hard" skills and why they need to be improved to gain sales excellence. In this chapter, we will identify, practice, and apply key techniques of account research, selling to the C-level, and a growth plan that is easy to follow and apply. Planning ahead is an ongoing activity that ensures that each sales opportunity is qualified and winnable, keeping the application of valuable resources efficient, focused, and effective.

These skills are also required today to filter your data to ensure accuracy before it goes into your CRM (Customer Reltionshp Manager) and automation systems. The data from the planning techniques go into the prioritized key accounts planning tool, and that tool acts as a critical filter and bolt-on for all your data input to your CRM and automation systems. This chapter ends with a focus on learning how to apply these unique sales excellence planning techniques and tools linked to practical exercises so that you can use them as filters or in parallel to integrate them into the CRM and sales process to ensure your deal is real and your data input is correct.

Techniques: Business Planning: Key Activities

- Have You Completed Your Plan? If it's not written down it will not happen!
- Are you aligned with your customer or prospective buyer? Do you know their issues?

Remember, in Chapter 2, we identified and discussed that the most important principle is to align your activities with that of your buyer and stakeholders. So, the following activities must be aligned. The techniques and tools that follow will help you achieve that aim.

> Buyer activities: Agreed company and personal key performance indicators
> Seller activities: Plan territory and prioritize key accounts
> CRM stage: Business planning/noticing/identifying
> SALES GOAL: Be on quota and have up-to-date territory and account growth plans

Business Planning Techniques Checklist

Ask yourself these critical questions. Have you… :

- Agreed on clear and measurable business goals with your manager?
- Completed a health check to know where you really are now?
- Knowledge of the required pipeline and win rate to reach quarterly/annual quota?
- Recorded daily, weekly, monthly activities in your CRM and/or selling diary?
- Completed in-depth research on existing and potential new accounts?
- Recorded an action plan in each defined territory and industry segment?
- Recorded results in CRM and/or selling diary, amended actions as required?

If you can honestly answer 'Yes' to all the above questions, then you can start to develop your business and prepare to start selling. If you answer 'No' to any one of the above questions, then you are at risk of not achieving your true sales potential. Remember the old saying in sales … 'Fail to Plan then Plan to Fail!'

These planning techniques will help you develop your skills:

- **Account research**

- **C-level executive sales research and checklist**
- **Growth plan**

Account Research (See Figure 3.1)

Before you do any sales calls on your prospective customers, you must do research and collect key data. This planning template on how to apply account research provides questions and data that you must research on four critical topics.

1. Prospect company insights
2. Strategic vendors
3. Industry information
4. Key people in the account

Insight is achieved by gaining knowledge from account research in the four areas identified in Figure 3.1. For example, if a company hasn't generated a net profit for several years, then this is a serious problem for any company. You can find out the net profit of any company by reading the annual report and their summaries for public companies. For private companies, you must read the financial report sections of industry-standard research companies online that will provide the data. Your key activity is to work out how resolving the customer's business problem with your technology can remove the problem and achieve the business outcome all the executives desire, but you must also combine that with insight statements that demonstrate how your solution can

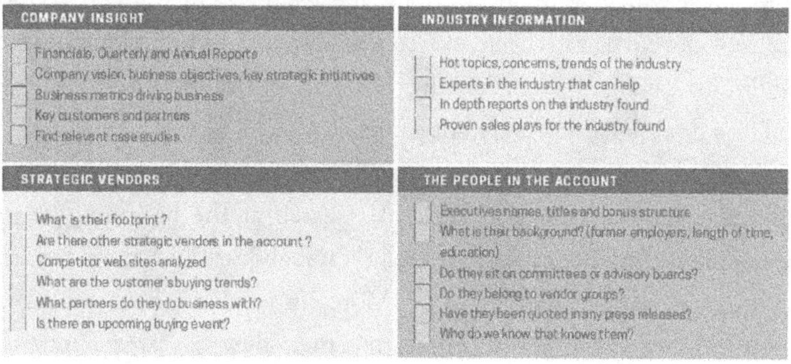

COMPANY INSIGHT
- Financials, Quarterly and Annual Reports
- Company vision, business objectives, key strategic initiatives
- Business metrics driving business
- Key customers and partners
- Find relevant case studies

INDUSTRY INFORMATION
- Hot topics, concerns, trends of the industry
- Experts in the industry that can help
- In depth reports on the industry found
- Proven sales plays for the industry found

STRATEGIC VENDORS
- What is their footprint?
- Are there other strategic vendors in the account?
- Competitor web sites analyzed
- What are the customer's buying trends?
- What partners do they do business with?
- Is there an upcoming buying event?

THE PEOPLE IN THE ACCOUNT
- Executives names, titles and bonus structure
- What is their background? (former employers, length of time, education)
- Do they sit on committees or advisory boards?
- Do they belong to vendor groups?
- Have they been quoted in any press releases?
- Who do we know that knows them?

Figure 3.1 Account research

also be linked to improving their net profit and achieve their company and personal goals.

Account research and understanding the C-level executives individual business needs and applying that knowledge interactively during the whole sales process from planning to confirming each sale will drive successful sales results and will help grow your own business and that of your customers. The growth results from using the knowledge gained in good planning to change the prospecting capabilities in order to be able to pinpoint and target genuine-quality opportunities based on the real success achieved. Basing prospecting on leads generated, size of prospect, sellers wish-full thinking, or targeting market leaders in your industry often wastes valuable selling time. Prospecting must be based on knowing how your solution generates real, relevant customer-desired business outcomes.

Case Study: Account Research

The European Mercedes Dealership

I was coaching a very capable sales team who were in the process of selling their human resources (HR) and payroll solution to one of Europe's largest Mercedes dealerships. Everything was going well. The sale was accurately forecasted, and the business outcomes and technical capabilities had all been identified, proven, and accepted. However, the executive board, especially the CEO, seemed unwilling to sign the purchase order and kept delaying the decision with last-minute objections, which were always overcome by the sales team. It seemed the key problem had been overcome, and the business outcome of significant savings by outsourcing HR and payroll was accepted, but still, the final signatures were not gained.

I asked the sales team to put themselves in the shoes of each executive. Go back to their account research at the beginning of the sale. What did the executives really care about? Did they feel the reward was higher than the risk? More importantly, how were they rewarded financially? For example, together, they all cared about the health of the company and wanted to resolve problems blocking their business objectives, but their personal needs and goals and how they are rewarded were also important, but each was different. For example, the chief technical officer (CTO) had to be sure the solution solved the company technical problems, but he also needed to gain his annual bonus, and he felt the risk of losing his bonus was still too high. The chief operating officer (COO), who had HR and payroll responsibility, had to be sure of the increase in operational efficiency but wanted to be sure it would also result in her receiving her bonus. The chief executive officer (CEO) was bonused entirely on net profit. This insight was gained from their annual report and quarterly business public declarations in their finance world. All the CEO cared about was the net profit of the company and getting his large bonus based on the net profit achieved. The CEO could see how saving hundreds of thousands provided savings and rewards for the chief information officer(CIO), CTO, and COO, but the savings were planned to be spent on their pet projects. He was worried that the net profit would not increase or affect his annual bonus.

I asked the sales team leader and key account manager to add a specific section to the proposal and present it directly to the CEO and board. They felt it outside the remit of their role as a technical and software company. I pointed out while it was critical to link their technical capability to the desired business outcome of the prospective company, they must also link that to each executive's business rewards. The team thought it was very bold but decided it was appropriate given the circumstances, and the relationship with the board executives was good. The sales team boldly suggested a variety of possible application of the savings from the project. One of these was the suggestion that the savings could be used to purchase 300 more cars, which would generate 28 percent net profit. The efficiencies gained from the technology had been difficult to demonstrate in the ROI business case, but this suggestion immediately resonated, especially with the CEO. His focus had always been on net profit, and all he ever thought about was cars and the profit made from each car sold. The objections to the sale evaporated, and the purchase order was quickly approved by the board.

Figure 3.2 Executive sales checklist

Selling to the C-Level

The biggest opportunities are found when you are in front of C-level executives. It may surprise you that this technique is contained in this business planning section. This is because it is essential you know all about the company and industry the executive is engaged in and how they are actively committed to achieve their own personal and business objectives. Planning in advance for your call and researching data on the executives is imperative. This interactive checklist template in Figure 3.2 on how to get to this level and apply this technique successfully will ensure you know the seven key steps to achieve the goal of being able to meet and engage with C-level executives and be of value to them. This means you will be able to provide key business insights to be able to tell them something they don't know about their company to build a strong trusting relationship and ultimately win more sales.

There are seven key data points in the research you need to perform with seven required checklists items.

1. **Identify the relevant executives by researching all available data online.**
   a. Have you identified the executive that stands to gain the most or lose the most because of your solution?
2. **Determine the best approach to get to the relevant executive.**

    a. Do you have a recommendation from a credible source within the prospect's own organization? Research from salesforce.com reveals that 84 percent of executives will then grant you a meeting.

    b. Do you have a referral from outside the organization? Research reveals that 50 percent of executives will then grant you a meeting

    c. Do you have a powerful pitch with WIFMs (What's In It For Me)? Only 20 percent will accept a cold call and grant you a meeting according to the research, so you need leverage and a recommendation.

3. **Perform the appropriate research before that critical first meeting.**

    a. Do you have an in-depth understanding of the key issues facing the executive?

    b. Do you have an in-depth understanding of their biggest block to achieving their key performance objectives?

    c. Are you confident you have done your full research before meeting the executive?

4. **Conduct an effective first meeting with the client executive.**

    a. Are you prepared to focus to begin to create a lasting longer-term relationship, not a short-term product or services sale?

5. **Demonstrate insight, integrity, and capability in subsequent meetings.**

    a. Are you able to demonstrate insight and expertise, capability and integrity?

6. **Executives must perceive you as a trusted advisor.**

    a. Have you demonstrated insight and expertise with capability and integrity that will lead to a collaborative relationship, so you operate in the client value zone?

7. **Consistently communicate your value to the executive.**

    a. At the end of each appointment with an executive and before you leave the call, you must agree on next steps. Agree on a date to meet up to review the proposed solution with

THE **SIX** KEY COMPONENTS OF A PLAN:

TIME	GOALS	STRATEGIES	ACTIONS	OBSTACLES	DEVELOPMENT
WHAT TIME SCALES ARE YOU WORKING TO? 'THE WHEN'	WHAT ARE YOU GOING TO ACHIEVE? 'THE WHAT'	HOW ARE YOU GOING TO DO IT? 'THE HOW'	LIST SPECIFIC SALES ACTIVITIES YOU WILL COMMIT TO.	WHAT IS IN THE WAY? FAILURE IS NOT AN OPTION, DON'T BELIEVE IN EXCUSES	HOW ARE YOU GOING TO GROW THIS YEAR? WHAT AREAS NEED DEVELOPMENT?

CREATE A PLAN!
People who write down their goals and plans are more successful than those who don't

TIME WHEN?	GOALS WHAT?	STRATEGIES HOW?	ACTIONS	OBSTACLES	DEVELOPMENT

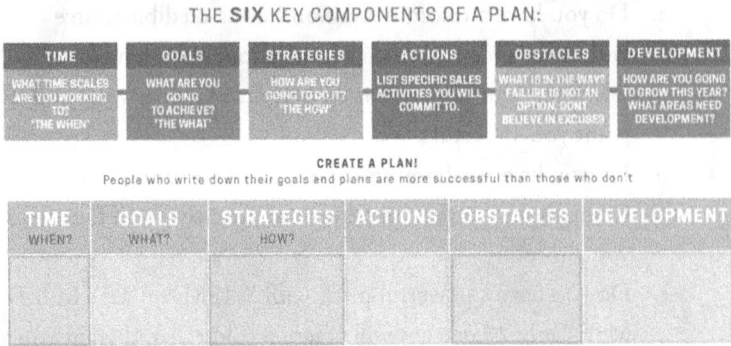

Figure 3.3 Growth plan

an executive and confirm with them the value that your solution will deliver to them and their company.

Growth Plan (See Figure 3.3)

CREATE A PLAN!

People who write down their goals and plans are more successful than those who don't. There are six key steps to achieve effective growth planning (Figure 3.3).

1. Timeline
2. Goals
3. Strategies
4. Actions
5. Obstacles
6. Development

Apply the series of questions to each item of your plan. It is important you fill in as much detail as you can. Be honest with yourself. If you don't know the answer, then find out. This will help you create a winning growth plan that builds you a winning sales plan that helps achieve your sales targets. Combine this technique with the account prioritizing tool in the next section, and you will achieve and sustain sales excellence.

Tool: Business Planning

Now that you have learned and practiced the planning techniques, it is time to input that data into your planning and account prioritizing sales tool. This tool will be with you throughout your sales year and is critically important in driving sales productivity of your CRM and sales automation. The tool ensures you respond and manage only the accounts with real spending potential. It will stop you and your manager from rushing resources into hot leads, for example, from a marketing campaign, that will ultimately keep slipping every quarter or will be lost and not drive the revenue you need. The tool achieves this by automatically prioritizing the importance of each account or opportunity by applying a deeply researched list of criteria that gives a score to each account and so prioritizes them in order of importance based on the size of the revenue opportunity and not, for example, based on the size of account's annual turnover.

First, you must complete a set of questions to establish what stage you are at in your planning efforts. This checklist will ensure you are ready to sell to the right customers at the right time throughout the year. If you can answer all the questions with "Yes," then you are in a good place and can move on to finding new business using the techniques and tools in the next chapter about prospecting. If any one of these answers is "No," then you must go to the planning tools and techniques and fix the issue. You will not gain sales excellence unless you do this task honestly and regularly throughout the year.

Business Planning Tool Checklist

Ask yourself these critical questions. Have you… :

- Completed your territory on-quota health check to identify gaps?
- Written down your resulting action plan and agreed with your manager?
- Created a territory and industry segmentation plan?
- Created a new business account growth plan?

- Identified the required pipeline to close revenue and quota gap?
- Calculated your personal conversion win rate and can track it?
- Identified your installed base, contacted, supported, and updated?
- Targeted your growth Industries, researched key accounts and opportunities?

If you can honestly answer "Yes" to all the above questions, then you can start to develop your business and prepare to start prospecting and selling. If you answer "No" to any one the above questions, then you are at risk of not achieving your true sales potential.

Remember the old saying in sales, fail to plan, then plan to fail. This planning tool method will deliver an effective plan (Figure 3.4).

These three key growth criteria factors are subdivided into 10 growth criteria as shown in Figure 3.5. These are based on feedback from surveys to over 4,000 attendees at nearly 300 SalesTechnique workshops over the last 15 years. As you can see, the questions are very specific and can only be answered Good/Poor, High/Low, or Yes/No, giving 1 point for positives and 0 for negatives.

Now you must complete the questions by inputting the number one or a two into the prioritize accounts tool. This action will automatically calculate the total for each account and then put them in order of importance to you. The list was in a random order at first until we

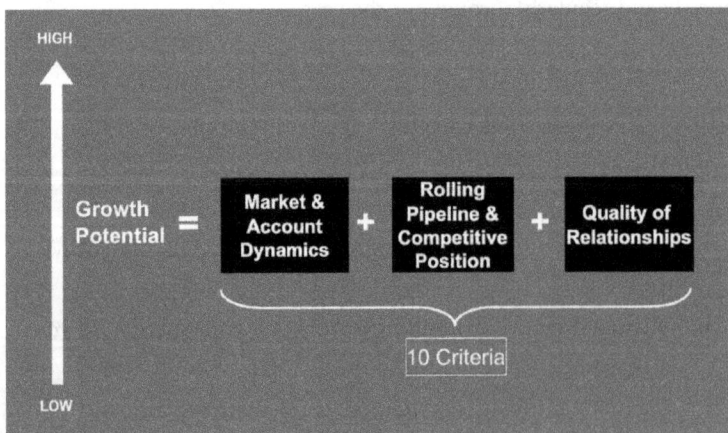

Figure 3.4 Assessing growth potential

Market & Account Dynamics	1) **Account Profile**; Performance (Growth/Profitability), Trends, Recent M&A and/or reorganizations	Good = 1	
		Poor = 0	
	2) **Market Growth**; Economic Climate, Competitive Position, Long-Term & Short-Term Growth Potential	High = 1	
		Low = 0	
	3) **Known demand for your Product & Solutions** (Brand Specific Readiness)	Yes = 1 (In Pipeline?)	
		No = 0	
Rolling Pipeline & Competitive Position	4) **Quality & value/volume of Pipeline** (any big deals on the horizon??)	Gross 2 / 3 x "Target" = 1	
		If not = 0	
	5) **Potential Growth**; Trends in IT (Software) Spending	High = 1	
		Low = 0	
	6) **Wallet Share**; Available Spend, your Product & Solution Share, Competitions Share (Distribution thereof)	If > 20% = 1	
		Otherwise = 0	
	7) **Your Company, Product & Solution Strength vs. Competition**	We dominate = 1	
		Competition dominate = 0	
Quality of Relationships	8) **Track Record**; Reference Account, Value delivered in the past ? Credibility ? Track Record such that it will drive incremental business in the next 12 months ?	Success stories/proven business cases available = 1	
		Otherwise = 0	
	9) **Quality of Relationships**; will it drive incremental business the next 12 months ? Cxx level support, Mentors ?	Exec Sponsorship = 1	
		Otherwise = 0	
	10) **Partners**; Aligned with Consultant/ Partners, willing to act on your behalf ? Partners position such that it will help incremental business the next 12 months ?	Yes = 1	
		No = 0	

Figure 3.5 Growth criteria

applied the tool. Each account now has a score per criterion according to the knowledge of you, the key account manager. It does not take long to complete this tool. However, this tool often reveals the enormous lack of unknown knowledge that exists, but then you can do something about it in a structured way. Once this task is completed, it means your accounts are in order of importance to you as you prospect for new business within your accounts and the data are accurate. The tool can add significantly to your account knowledge and transform your results and revenue stream, not to mention making the CRM more accurate.

There is an exercise at the end of this chapter that encourages you to download the tool and apply it to your key accounts.

Case Study: Prioritizing Accounts Tool

How Planning Transformed the Seller and Sales Team Results

A key account manager in a global IT company, whom I coached early in his sales career, was struggling with his sales results, had a poor pipeline, and felt he was not adding value to his key accounts. Together, we transformed his successful win rate with these planning techniques and the tool. We also combined my coaching planning efforts with sessions on how to apply the Insight tool and techniques contained in

Chapter 6. Combining both tools and the techniques transformed his productivity and overall sales success, and he was awarded top seller status that year. He discovered that research and deep knowledge of his customers current and potential needs resulted in a massive improvement in his ability to understand the customer's issues, resolve them quicker, prioritize his activities, and reduce time spent on unproductive activities. By combining that knowledge with the data and actions recommended by applying the insights tool in Chapter 6, he found that suddenly his customers valued him more, plus his CRM and sales forecasts became more accurate, predictable, and repeatable, so his managers also valued him more.

He is now a senior executive sales leader who still uses these tools and techniques to this day, producing accurate data that informs his CRM and AI systems. As a senior executive, he focuses on coaching and transferring these skills to his team, who are now all top performers.

How to Link Your Planning Activity to Your Prospecting Activity

You have completed your plan, done research on your existing key accounts, and worked out a script on how to get to see C-level executives and what to say when you get there. Now you must work out how to prospect for new business within these accounts. You need proven prospecting techniques within key accounts. However, when you are solely a new business account seller, it is no different. You need similar prospecting techniques, but they are now even more critical to your success because you cannot rely on repeat business from your existing accounts as a key account manager. A new business seller is often referred to as a hunter, while an account manager may be referred to as a farmer. This can be a useful analogy. Both are essential to survival, but each requires a different approach and a different type of sales personality and attitude. The new business seller must enjoy and be motivated by the word No! They must enjoy rejection and treat every sale as a personal challenge. They both need patience, but the account manager requires to be seen more as a team player from within both the potential customer and his own company. Successful account managers tend to possess more diplomacy skills, take a longer-term view of progress, and know how to apply their deep knowledge of teamwork. Successful new business sellers tend to be more laser-targeted and obsessed on achieving their new sales. Good ones avoid any distraction at all from that goal, which often means they are not team players. However, both need to have completed their plan, which must be linked to their prospecting activities. The following section demonstrates how to apply key prospecting techniques.

CHAPTER 4

Business Development

How to Gain New Business

In Chapter 2, we identified the eight 'hard' skills and why they need to be improved to gain sales excellence. In this chapter, we will identify, practice, and apply the key techniques of an interactive business development circle, a compelling sales call story, and a prospecting activity schedule that is easy to follow and apply. These techniques will guarantee that your sales opportunities are real, valuable, and winnable. The data from the prospecting techniques go into the prospecting tool and that tool acts as a critical filter and bolt-on for all your data input to your Customer Relationshio Management (CRM) and automation systems.Custom

Positive, regular prospecting for new business is the core activity of any salesperson and of any business enterprise. Without good-quality prospects, new business is hard to find, and often, the salespeople and the company start relying on squeezing as much as possible out of existing customers. The risk is then that all your sales opportunities are concentrated on a gradually reducing customer base, and losing one customer can bring down the whole company. Prospecting is an ongoing activity and should never stop.

This chapter ends with a focus on learning how to apply these unique sales excellence prospecting techniques and tools linked to practical exercises so that you can use them as filters or in parallel to integrate them into the CRM and sales process to ensure your data input is correct.

Business Development Prospecting: Key Activities

- Have you found new business prospects? New business is the heartbeat of business.
- Are you aligned with your customers' or prospects' business? Do you know their issues?
- Is your pipeline data in your CRM accurate, winnable, and reflect real revenue value?

The most important principle is to align your activities with that of your buyer and stakeholders. In your prospecting activities, you need to be aware that your potential customer has already identified and is analyzing the impact of any blockages to stop them from achieving their key strategic business objectives (SBOs). The potential blockages are what you need to have discovered before you approach your potential customer or if you have a hot lead from marketing. The following techniques and tools will help you achieve that aim.

Buyer activities: Analyze impact of business issues and define strategic objectives

Seller activities: Build pipeline, and target new business and growth accounts

CRM stage: Business development/noticed/identified

SALES GOAL: Work your business plan to reach sales excellence

Sales Prospecting: Activities Checklist

- Created prospecting calendar and followed your prospecting plan?
- Created and practiced your compelling story?
- Researched target accounts for SBOs?
- Identified business problems blocking key performance indicators(KPIs) and SBOs?
- Identified opportunities you can win that have these business problems?
- Confirmed client vision and business pains linked to business problems?

- Aligned client vision to your company products, services, capabilities?

If you can honestly answer 'Yes I am" to all the aforementioned aforementioned activities, then you will possess a high-quality, full pipeline of potentially winnable opportunities. If you answer 'No" to any one of the previous questions, then it is likely you will have a poor-quality and low-volume pipeline of sales opportunities. You will inevitably focus your time and resources on a few large deals that help you reach your targets, if you win them. As the deals start slipping or disappearing, you will find that your motivation gradually reduces with a corresponding increase in the reasons given to your manager as to why you are not achieving your sales targets. Prospecting for new business is by far the hardest part of any sales process. Human beings are not built to like rejection. In sales, you must like rejection. In fact, the word "no" or "not right now" must motivate you to double your efforts. All top sellers know that, next to a good executable plan, achieving sales excellence depends on building a high-quality pipeline of genuine sales opportunities that are self-generated. Marketing creates sales opportunities, but these should be in addition to your own efforts.

If you feel that you need to improve, then perhaps the following techniques and exercises might help.

- **Business development circle**
- **Sales call story**
- **Activity schedule**

Build a Development Circle

The circle of business development activity shown in Figure 4.1 should never stop. Being proactive at this stage of your prospecting for new business is the real secret of creating a quality and full pipeline. You need to know 'who' to talk to, 'how' to create the activity to find them, 'connect' to those resources you need, and know 'what' to say when you get in front of prospective customers, either online or face-to-face. It really does matter what you say from the very first contact with a prospect or existing customer. It is my coaching and management

Figure 4.1 Business development circle

experience that many sellers do not have enough deep information before first contact, nor do they have a well-prepared and rehearsed sales story. Your potential customer or existing customer will not forgive you for not knowing their business, their industry, and something about their issues. If you start by asking questions in today's world of accessible data, you will hit a roadblock or indeed be delegated to a junior colleague. You start by making a business insight and immediately being of value. More on that topic later in this chapter.

WHO to Talk to?

In the previous planning section, you decided what accounts to research and prospect and what trusted connections you needed in social networks, business partners, and in your wider company. Your actions should have included deep account research plus identifying the executives and the line of business managers. Critically, it is now time to create a rolling list of the top 20 prioritized targeted accounts. The planning tool in Chapter 3 explains how to achieve this objective and delivers an effective prioritized account list.

HOW do You Find Them?

You need to create a prospecting activity that is effective and works within your capabilities. The prospecting activity scheduler (Figure 4.3) described in detail, which follows the creating your sales story exercise later in this chapter, will deliver this prospecting activity plan for you.

CONNECTED to the Right Resources?

Is your LinkedIn profile effective? Are your social media links in place? Which business partners and vendors do you know and trust, and do they trust you? Have you reached out to them recently? How well-connected are you to your internal company team? Are you important to them, why and how? These are just a few of the essential connections you need internally and externally. I have assumed you are already very effective at this skill. If you are struggling, then you need to learn how to improve your online presence and profile. It is not the objective of this book to help you learn how to use today's social media apps and online resources. However, I have referenced many good books and links to great resources to help you achieve these goals in the Appendix pages.

WHAT do You Say?

It is what you say and what you do when you get in front of the prospective customer, face-to-face or virtually, that matters most. You need a good, compelling sales story that you can confidently deliver by phone, email, social media, virtually, and face-to-face. A suggested approach to creating your own powerful sales story comes next.

Create Your Sales Call Story

One of the most essential and critical skills that any sales professional needs to develop, practice, and be able to apply is to deliver a compelling and convincing sales story. Your prospective customer needs a reason to listen to you and act with you.

Do this activity well, and you will create a critical sales asset that drives your confidence, increases the number of sales opportunities, and delivers and exceeds your planned revenue. Do it badly or ignore this vital activity, and you will find your confidence being gradually sucked away as each contact, lead, or opportunity you approach refuses to continue discussions after first contact or will not even agree to an appointment to talk.

Your Sales Story Is not About You

Prospective customers are not interested in what you do; they are only interested in what you can do for them. In other words, no one cares how smart you are or how great you think your company is. They want to know what's in it for them.

We all think WIFM (what's in it for me). It's an important survival technique and human basic instinct. So, stop talking about yourself and your company and begin by leading with the issues, pains, problems, opportunities, and results that are important to your prospect. People, companies, and prospects have needs. The job of sales is to connect with customers and prospective customers to determine if your solutions will meet their needs.

You must be seen as someone who is bringing "value" to them individually and to their business. All research and experience show that the most successful sellers tend to be the most active. However, it is what you say when you get there that matters the most. Real business issues and hot topics always get you a first meeting.

As you can see in Figure 4.2, there are eight elements to creating a good sales story.

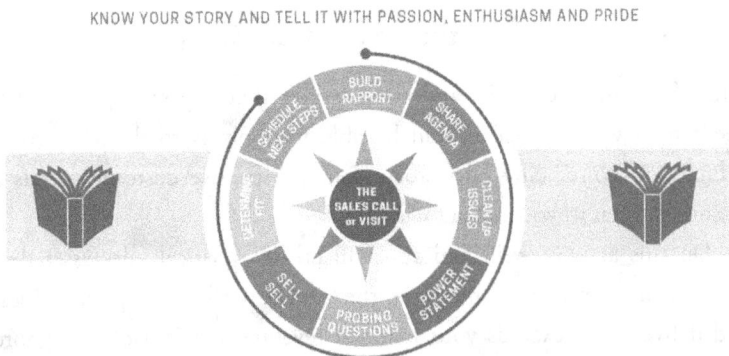

KNOW YOUR STORY AND TELL IT WITH PASSION, ENTHUSIASM AND PRIDE

Figure 4.2 Create your sales call story

I.   BUILD RAPPORT to IDENTIFY BUYERS STYLE
   * Engage buyer in everyday conversation, smile, connect,
     practice mirroring, adapt.

II. SHARE AGENDA to GET BUY IN and SEEK INPUT
   * It is a big differentiator—"this is what I was looking to do in
     our time together today." It informs the buyer where you are
     headed, provides road map, feels more comfortable. It lets
     the buyer know that you expect a dialogue and surprises the
     buyer with your solid plan.

III. CLEAN UP ISSUES (EXISTING CUSTOMERS ONLY)
   * Deal with the junk up front if this is an existing customer.
     Clear the air. Keep your promises

IV. POWER STATEMENT DELIVERED (TELL YOUR STORY
     —in 3 MINUTES)
   * Deliver a succinct, compelling, client—focused understand-
     ing of why this type of company come to your company,
     what you offer, and how you are different from, and
     better than other alternatives. Watch and listen carefully for
     physical reactions and verbal signs that you have hit a nerve
     or a salient point. For example, they write something down
     or ask you a question. Be patient. Keep your powder dry.
     DO NOT launch into a full-blown sales pitch.

V.   PROBING QUESTIONS to DISCOVER BUSINESS PAINS.
   * Personal questions: what is personally important to your
     potential customer? (WIFM's) Strategic and directional
     questions. Find out and discuss what is taking place in
     clients world. (pre-call research). Specific issue seeking
     and opportunity seeking questions; pains, problems, needs,
     desires. These are critical sales process questions to get you to
     the destination. For example, a pilot needs to know about air
     traffic, weather, flight plan and so on.

VI. SELL, SELL, SELL
   * Now it's your turn. Tie in buyer's needs, issues, opportunities
     into your offerings

- Tailor your message to the needs of your prospect. Pull out literature, review charts and graphs, share stories of helping clients, show off latest product or service and best customer testimonials. However, do not present yet or do a demonstration. **Discovery always precedes presentation or pricing.**

VII DETERMINE FIT AND SEEK OUT OBJECTIONS

- You might say, based on our conversation and what we've shared with each other, it looks like we might be a fit to help you.

VII DEFINE AND SCHEDULE THE NEXT STEPS

- At the end of the call, you would say: What do you suggest as an appropriate next step? Grab a phone calendar, agree it, book it.

Example

Here is an example of a good, shared agenda in a sales call.

Tom, thanks for inviting me in. I believe we set up this meeting for thirty minutes. How are you on time? (pause for the answer). Great. I will make sure we are done before 11.30.

Here's what I would like to do. Let me kick us off and take just two or three minutes to share a bit about SBI, the issues we solve for IT professionals, and why they tend to bring us in for help. I will also touch briefly on how we are different and why we have been so successful in this space. Then I'd like to turn it around and ask you questions to understand more about your situation and what you are doing regarding the move from traditional infrastructure to the Cloud and Hybrid combinations in between. How you are dealing with issues on network, infrastructure, collaboration and applications, mobile technology and IT security services.

Depending on what I hear from you, I can share a few relevant case studies or show you options for how we provide IT managed services for our clients. After that, we can discuss if it looks like we might be a fit together to help you or if there is a logical next step

(such as whether it makes sense to have a follow up meeting or get our teams together)

That is what I was hoping to do, Tom. Please tell me what you were hoping for and what you would like to walk away with today?

Exercise

Now let's do a quick exercise to get you started.

STEP 1. Brainstorm with your company colleagues to create a list of answers to these questions.
- Why did your best customers initially come to you?
- What business problems were they facing?
- What results were they looking to achieve?
- What pains are your potential customers likely to experience?
- What problems do you see prospects experiencing from trying to do it for themselves that you should be handling for them?
- What is the potential cost to them of not working with you?
- Why do your existing customers still do business with you?

STEP 2. Create three pages of blank paper and head them
- Page 1. Client issues
- Page 2. Offerings
- Page 3. Differentiators

Now using these answers on Page 1, craft a client issues summary statement. Try to incorporate compelling, emotional, or provocative words or phrases to describe your client's experiences. For example, customers are exhausted, frustrated, pressured, and so on, from trying to achieve a business result. Put it in phrases that speak to the business issues that your prospect addresses, and be careful not to list reasons your company is so wonderful.

On Page 2, list what you are offering. Should be easy.

On Page 3, list the reasons that you believe your prospects, products, services, and/or solutions are better and different, for example, technical, cultural, proprietary processes, service, guarantees, the salespeople.

Now craft a compelling statement by combining all three pages in a sequence. You should now have a succinct, compelling, customer-focused understanding and statement of WHY companies come to you and your company, WHAT you offer, and HOW you are different from, and better than, other competing alternatives.

Activity Schedule

You must have a daily, weekly, monthly, and quarterly written down prospecting schedule. First, to have a realistic schedule of daily prospecting in your calendar that meets your revenue targets, you need to calculate how many calls you need to make and how many meetings you need to get the right number of qualified opportunities and proposals. Finally, you need to know how many deals you need annually to be on quota. I have created a simple tool that will automatically calculate these numbers. All you need to do is enter your quota, your average deal size, and your win rate. An example of this popular and highly successful activity schedule with a suggested spreadsheet and template is in Figure 4.3.

In the Appendix, there is a link that you can use to download this very helpful prospecting technique and tool. Once downloaded, you can follow the instructions or contact me, details are in the Appendix.

	EXAMPLES					
Quota (£ k gm)	£1,200,000	£1,200,000	£1,200,000	£1,200,000	£1,200,000	
Average Deal Size (£ k)	£20,000	£50,000				
Won Deals Needed Annually	60	24				To reduce this the average deal size needs to be increased
Win Rate	25%	25%	25%	25%	25%	
Proposals Required	240	96				To reduce this the wins rate needs to be increased
Opportunities Qualified	320	128				Research proves that 75% of qualified opportunities move to proposal
Initial Meetings Needed	481	193				Research proves that 66% of initial meetings then move to prospects stage
Proactive Conversations Needed	962	386				Research proves that 50% of proactive conversations then turn into first initial meetings

Figure 4.3 Complete your activity schedule

How to Use This Technique to Create an Effective Prospecting Activity Schedule

1. Data input is required only in the pink or yellow boxes. The tool then automatically calculates the outcomes from your data input to guide your action plan.

2. Add your annual quota or gross margin target to the top line in the five boxes.

3. Add your minimum and maximum deal size from lowest to highest in the five boxes based on your own CRM history.

4. The tool automatically works out for you the number of deals you need to win annually per deal size. You will immediately realize that increasing the deal size reduces the number you need to close every year.

5. You must now add your current win rate percentage. This is calculated by looking back at your sales history and dividing your actual forecasted sales number in a full year by your actual sales wins. You must be honest. Don't guess this win rate percentage number. Do not just add your pipeline as your forecast number. You must use your actual forecast numbers that you gave to your sales manager.

6. The tool now works out the number of proposals required. This will surprise and possibly shock you. Figure 4.3 demonstrates that the lower your average deal size is, the higher the number of proposals you require. For example, at 20,000 deal value, at a win rate of 25 percent, you will need 240 proposals. Contrast that with an average deal size of 50,000 with the same win rate of 25 percent, which requires only 96 proposals annually. The next chapter explains in detail and provides the tools on how to increase your win rate and your deal size in any company and with any product.

7. Sales research from Salesforce.com has revealed that 75 percent of qualified opportunities move to proposal stages. So, the tool has calculated the number of opportunities you require for each scenario that you find yourself in. For example, to achieve 48 proposals, you need 64 opportunities. However, if you have not

qualified your prospects effectively, then the number of proposals you need is much, much higher. Check out the qualification techniques in this chapter and the qualification tools in the next chapter. In addition, if your win rate also goes down, then you need to increase your number of opportunities. When you change your win rate in the tool, it will recalculate the required numbers.

8. Sales research has also revealed that 66 percent of initial meetings with executives, influencers, and sponsors result in moving to opportunity stage. For example, in Figure 4.3, the tool quickly reveals that you need 481 meetings to get at least 320 qualified opportunities if your deal size is small and 25 meetings to get 16 opportunities if your deal size is large.

9. Sales research reveals that 50 percent of proactive conversations turn into first initial meetings. In Figure 4.3, you can see that if your deal size remains low relative to your annual target, then you will need an astonishing 962 real effective conversations to get 481 meetings to get 320 opportunities to get 240 proposals, and at a win rate of 25 percent, you will have to win 60 deals annually!! In contrast, even with the same annual target, you will reach that annual target if you increase your deal size or increase your win rate. With the same annual target, a seller with an average deal size increased to 50,000 dramatically reduces their required calls and conversations to 386, resulting in 193 initial meetings, 128 opportunities, and 96 proposals at a win rate of 25 percent, and will only need 24 deals won annually.

The objective of this great combined tool and technique is to provide you with a reality check and demonstrate how effective you need to be to have any chance of meeting your targets and quotas. The tool sits alongside your CRM and is an effective bolt-on and filter to move you in the right direction. It stops you from assuming that everything is ok and critically provides the data to link to the other tools in this book that will help you find prospects, qualify effectively, and then actively progress your deals to win more sales and consistently reach your annual targets.

Business Prospecting Tool Checklist

Ask yourself these critical questions. Have you... :

- Developed deep knowledge of target industries and growth enterprises?
- Created the planned numbers of prospects for your pipeline?
- Created a compelling sales story that will build trust with prospects?
- Identified your prospects business pains and business objectives?
- Uncovered the factors driving prospects business changes?
- Achieved a network of required people inside and outside the company?
- Identified the required company, supplier, and/or business partner resources?
- Quantified the prospecting metrics and account growth criterion?

If you can honestly answer 'Yes' to all the above questions, then you can start qualifying your prospects that have come from your own efforts or indeed from marketing campaigns, social media, and websites. If you answer 'No' to any one of the previous questions, then it is likely you will have a poor-quality and low-volume pipeline of sales opportunities. Your action now is to combine the previous prospecting techniques, especially the activity scheduler, with the prospecting tool.

Business Prospecting Tool: Pipeline Growth

This prospecting tool is a direct extension of the accounts prioritizing planning tool in Chapter 3. There is the usual section on account and market dynamics, but then the next sections are different. Reference ability, networking, finance, industry differentiator, pipeline, and details to find are added. The scoring system is the same as the accounts prioritize tool. The input of values in the finance section should be self-explanatory. Once this task is completed, then you need to check your data before you input to your CRM. It is, however, an optional task, and many find it is too complicated for them and probably unnecessary. My suggestion at the of this chapter is try the planning tool in Chapter 3, and if you find that helpful, then download this prospecting tool from the Appendix and give it a try.

Case Study Finding the Golden Nuggets

Building Sales Confidence

I was coaching a major UK plc company with 75 salespeople and discovered that their confidence was lower than expected. I also noticed that their pipeline and closing rates were gradually diminishing. The company had an inside sales team driving new business, but the key major account salespeople seemed to be struggling to get new opportunities within their key accounts. I asked one team to present to me as if I was their prospective customer. Their sales story was all about how wonderful their technology was and that their company was a leader in their market. I arranged a workshop for all the key account managers. We created a great sales story with each salesperson using the technique explained in Figure 4.2. They revised their sales story regularly. Practiced it on each other and became an expert at telling it with passion, enthusiasm, and pride. Their story was based not on technology but focused on what they could do for their customer's business.

We then combined the planning tool with the prospecting tool and created strategies that laser-targeted opportunities within their key accounts that they had either not followed up or had not known about until they approached their key account contacts with their new sales story. I can honestly report that these simple activities during the workshops, which they then applied enthusiastically, tripled their opportunities within their key accounts and doubled their pipeline. As a direct result of taking the teams out of the field for a few days and applying these techniques and tools, their confidence soared, and so did their results.

CHAPTER 5

Opportunity Identification

How to Gain Real Opportunities

In Chapter 2, we identified the eight 'hard' skills and why they need to be improved to gain sales excellence. In this chapter, we will identify, practice, and apply the key techniques of the most important activity of all the sales skills. The sales profession calls this skill qualifying the opportunity. Not qualifying your opportunity is the main cause of lost or slipped sales.

Any salesperson or manager reading this chapter will know, deep down, that this is where most opportunities are lost and won. In my experience, every time a deal slips or is lost, when we analyze where it went wrong, the conclusion is almost always we did not qualify the sales opportunity, and perhaps we should never have invested all the valuable resources in the first place. It should be the first step taken by any salesperson, but in today's business world, the buyer has already done most of his research on you and your products and often starts his buying journey by sending you a request for pricing. The attraction of getting a deal from a good opportunity that you did not know about often blinds salespeople to the reality that the sale is not qualified, and you might be getting used as quote fodder. Most sales organizations and salespeople work on the principle of being incredibly positive and hopeful, but that is not a helpful way to approach a new opportunity. Being careful and being a skeptic is a better approach than being hopeful and positive. This is highlighted by one of my favorite authors, Rick Page, in his book *Hope Is Not a Strategy*. At this stage of any sale, the ability to be realistic, blunt, cynical, and to doubt everything you hear and read is critical.

These techniques will guarantee that your sales opportunities are real, valuable, and winnable.

The data from the qualifying techniques go into the opportunity metrics tool, and that tool acts as a critical filter and bolt-on for all your data input to your Customer Relationship Management (CRM) and automation systems. Positive, regular qualification of potential new business is the core activity of any salesperson and of any business enterprise. Without good-quality, qualified prospects, new business opportunities will not happen when forecasted because the salespeople will often go ahead and demonstrate their product or solution, provide prices and proposals much too early in the process.

This chapter ends with a focus on learning how to apply these sales excellence qualifying techniques and tools linked to practical exercises so that you can use them as filters or in parallel to integrate them into the CRM and sales process to ensure your data input is correct.

Opportunity Identification Qualification: Key Activities

- Is your opportunity real or wishful thinking? Should you apply valuable resources?
- Are you aligned with your buyer who is looking at the impact of his problem?
- Are you confident you can turn this opportunity into revenue and win this sale?

The most important principle is to align your activities with that of your buyer and stakeholders. In your qualifying activities, you need to be aware that your potential customer has already developed their plan and has identified and analyzed the impact of any blockages to stop them from achieving their key strategic business objectives. The next step they will already have completed is to initiate a project to remove the blockages. These potential blockages are what you need to have discovered when you were first researching and prospecting for new business, and now you need to identify, qualify, and quantify the financial impact of the blockages on their business. The following techniques and tools will help you achieve that aim.

Buyer activities: Agree plan, initiate project
Seller activities: Identify opportunities and create business insights
CRM stage: Identified/validating
SALES GOAL: Identify the buyers' desired business outcomes, the
   impact of buyers' business problems, and the cost of the business
   pains stopping those business outcomes.

You can start qualifying your prospects that have come from your own efforts or indeed from marketing campaigns, social media, and websites. In any business that is successful, the identification of blockages that stop the business from reaching the planned business outcome and expected profit is of the highest priority to the executives and buyers given the role of choosing a supplier. All else will be secondary. Solving and removing that blockage is critical. Consequently, identifying the same blockages is also of the highest priority for the seller.

In parallel, the business must also grow and develop, and so any product or service that accelerates the planned growth will be the highest priority and interest to the executives and buyers. However, due to the law of status quo, business issues that stop the business from achieving its key goal are of higher priority than just business growth. The salesperson must understand this fact, and to excel and differentiate themselves from the competition, the best strategy to achieve sales excellence is to offer a product or solution that both removes the blockages and increases growth to help achieve lower costs and higher revenue.

This means that opportunity identification and qualification are the most important and critical parts of any sales process, as they determine the ultimate outcome of the whole buyer–seller process and confirmed sale. Most sales research reveals and highlights that the reason why 75 percent of all sales opportunities are not sold is because, to quote a customer from the research; *"the sales organisation did not offer me a solution that fitted our business needs nor removed the business problems we were experiencing."* In fact, the most recent research reveals that the greatest difference between sales winners and second place finishers is the value they provide to buyers through insight, education, and collaboration, which is the key conclusion in the book *Insight Selling: Surprising Research on What Sales Winners Do Differently*: Schultz and Doer.

Opportunity Identification: Qualification Techniques Checklist

- Begun to uncover budget, authority, need, timeframe?
- Identified technical/business problems/pains blocking business objectives?
- Identified the compelling reason (or event) to act?
- Analyzed financial impact of client not resolving problems?
- Identified, quantify financial impact of business pains/business problems?
- Developed business insights, ideas, and perspectives for client?

If you can honestly answer 'Yes, I am doing this' to all the above activities, then you can start developing real business insight and discover what the key business problem is, how much it costs the company, and what impact it would have to remove the problem. If you cannot answer 'Yes' to all the above questions, then you are at risk of applying your skills more in hope than reality. Remember, hope is not a good strategy. Decide now to progress the sale based on reality not conjecture or driven by targets and managers.

If you feel that you need to improve, then perhaps the following techniques and exercises might help.

- **Qualify in/out**
- **Score opportunity**
- **Validate opportunity**

Qualify in or out

To help you decide if you should continue or start spending time qualifying a sales lead or a request from a prospect, here are a series of IN or OUT criteria based on a wide range of recent buyer research (Figure 5.1).

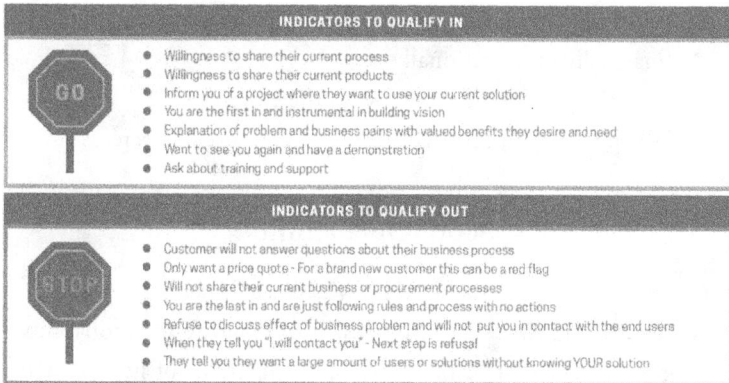

Figure 5.1 Qualify IN or OUT. The first step is to establish whether you should be involved in this prospective customer at all

INDICATORS TO QUALIFY IN and SPEND MORE TIME: If all boxes are ticked, then do proceed.

- Willingness to share their current process.
- Willingness to share their current products.
- Inform you of a project where they want to use your current solution.
- You are the first in and instrumental in building vision.
- Explanation of problem and business pains with valued benefits they desire and need.
- Want to see you again and have a demonstration.
- Ask about training and support.

INDICATORS TO QUALIFY OUT and MOVE ON: If YES, then DO NOT proceed.

- Customer will not answer questions about their business process.
- Only want a price quote—For a brand-new customer this can be a red flag.
- Will not share their current business or procurement processes.
- You are the last in, and so they are just following rules and processes with no intended actions.

- Refuse to discuss the effect of their business problem, either financially or operationally.
- Will not put you in contact with the end users.
- When they tell you, I will contact you. Next step is refusal.

Score Opportunity

One of the key steps in qualification, which is an essential activity before you start investing time and resources, is to quantify the probability of winning versus the cost of the opportunity in terms of its potential to your business. This helps make the decision whether to invest resources, and then if you continue, this action will increase the probability of winning the sale (Figure 5.2).

There are five key areas to investigate and establish a points score:

1. Organizational basics

   It seems obvious, but many people in sales at this early stage of their sales opportunity do not research, check, or ask their potential customer the direct question: Do you have the financial capability or budget to invest in resolving this problem you have presented? This is linked to the question which asks why it's a problem and what is the financial impact of the problem. If the

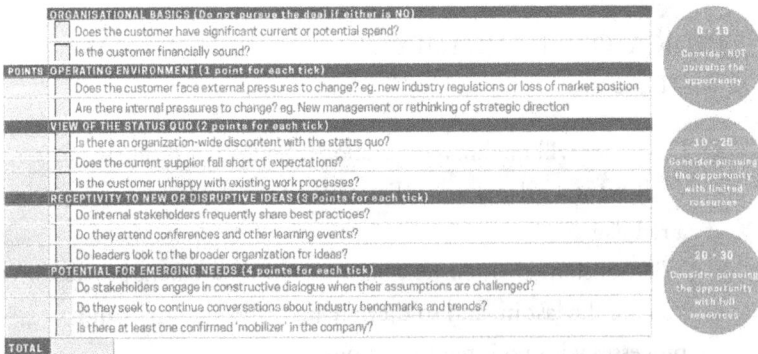

ORGANISATIONAL BASICS (Do not pursue the deal if either is NO)		
Does the customer have significant current or potential spend?		0 - 10
Is the customer financially sound?		Consider NOT
POINTS OPERATING ENVIRONMENT (1 point for each tick)		pursuing the opportunity
Does the customer face external pressures to change? eg. new industry regulations or loss of market position		
Are there internal pressures to change? eg. New management or rethinking of strategic direction		
VIEW OF THE STATUS QUO (2 points for each tick)		
Is there an organization-wide discontent with the status quo?		10 - 20
Does the current supplier fall short of expectations?		Consider pursuing
Is the customer unhappy with existing work processes?		the opportunity with limited
RECEPTIVITY TO NEW OR DISRUPTIVE IDEAS (3 Points for each tick)		resources
Do internal stakeholders frequently share best practices?		
Do they attend conferences and other learning events?		
Do leaders look to the broader organization for ideas?		20 - 30
POTENTIAL FOR EMERGING NEEDS (4 points for each tick)		Consider pursuing
Do stakeholders engage in constructive dialogue when their assumptions are challenged?		the opportunity with full
Do they seek to continue conversations about industry benchmarks and trends?		resources
Is there at least one confirmed 'mobilizer' in the company?		
TOTAL		

Figure 5.2 *Score the opportunity. How to quantify the opportunity to determine what level of resources is required in terms of its potential to win new business*

answer is No to this financial question, then do not pursue the opportunity. If the answer is Yes, then definitely proceed.

2. Operating environment

The most constant factor in our business and personal lives is change. Change drives actions and reactions. If there are no external or internal pressures to change in the potential customer's company or industry, then that gets no points. If there are clear and obvious pressures, then each gets a point.

3. View of the status quo

If there is a stable environment in the prospect's company, for example, the incumbent supplier is doing well, and the executives and front-line managers are happy, then unless there is pressure to change from another source, no points are given to these factors. However, if it is clear there is companywide discontent or process issues, and the current supplier is stated by the company executives to be poor, then points for each factor.

4. Receptive to new ideas

This is an area often not investigated and is critical to establishing need. If there is a reluctance to share practices, and the leaders do not attend or care about learning more about their industry either because they say they know everything or there is resistance to new ideas, then no points for this lack of factors and definite points if they are clearly motivated by new ideas.

5. Potential for emerging needs

Often salespeople state that the potential customer was not co-operative, and so sales managers blame the salesperson's lack of skill in asking questions and discovering issues. In fact, it points to a more likely scenario that the managers and executives are not aligned about the need for the project or recognition of the business problem's existence and importance. Scoring low in this area indicates that the prospect is not ready, so the sales organization needs to keep investment in resources to a minimum until the time is right to commit valuable resources. Scoring high in this area is a very good sign.

Adding up the scores in this model and technique gives a very accurate measurement of whether to invest time and resources in an opportunity, as shown in Figure 5.2. The model helps the sales management to decide the level of resources to invest, while indicating the potential for success or failure early in the sales process. Once again, by qualifying and measuring the opportunity early in the process, the chances of a delayed or slipped deal later are very much reduced. In addition, the data being put from these techniques into your CRM tool ensure the accuracy of predicting the results and determines the type of questions to ask your AI tools to help progress the deal.

Validate Opportunity

You need to make sure your opportunity is real and there is a reasonable chance you can win the sale. Write down your answers to the questions in the model shown in Figure 5.3.

The most important factor by far in making sure the opportunity is real, quantified, and measured is the answer to the question: What is the potential financial impact of the issues? Often the prospect does not even know, but very often the salesperson does not find out nor directly ask the right questions, so the sale progresses based on technical merit alone. This is often not enough to influence the C-level executives'

	QUESTIONS		ANSWERS	CHECK?
OBJECTIVE Complete the following	What is the Business Problem ?...and the associated Business Pain?			
	Which LOBs does this business problem impact?			
VALIDATE Do not proceed unless boxes are checked	In client terms what is the potential financial impact of:	The business pain?		
		Solving the business pain?		
		Doing Nothing?		
	Client sees the value of solving the business pain?			
	What is the implementation timeframe?			
OUTCOME Qualified with action plan	What is compelling reason to act or compelling event?			
	What is the anticipated buying process?			
	Will we win? What are your unique differentiators?			

Figure 5.3 Score the opportunity. How to quantify the opportunity to determine what level of resources is required in terms of its potential to win new business

decisions later in the sale. A business case may be done later, but often there are too much vested interests and politics at the later stage, so the answers are more guarded and biased. Best to work out the financial implications with the potential customer at the beginning.

1. What is the business problem and the associated business pain? Business problems and the business pain caused by the problems are not the same thing. For example, the problem might be that you are using an out-of-date software app, but the pain is the impact caused by constant errors caused by using that software.
2. Which line of business does this business problem impact?
3. In client terms, what is the potential financial impact of:
    a. The business pains?
    b. Solving the business pains?
    c. Doing nothing.
4. Does the client see the value of solving the business pain?
5. What is the implementation timeframe? What is the compelling reason to act or the compelling event?
6. What is the anticipated buying process?
7. Will we win? What are your unique differentiators?

If you can answer fully and honestly the above questions, then this creates an action plan, and your opportunity may be real, and it is worth allocating resources and progressing to discover what business problems the client seeks to solve. If you cannot answer all these questions, especially the potential financial impact, then consider not pursuing this opportunity at all. Alternatively, go back to the prospective customer and ask them all seven questions. If you receive all that data from them, they may well discover that they need to answer these questions before they proceed, and so you added value because you have helped them know what they don't know.

Opportunity Identification Qualification Tool Checklist

Ask yourself these critical questions. Have you:

- Agreed with buyers that we have the capability to solve technical/business problems?
- Identified the business problems blocking business objectives, and the buyer agrees?
- Quantified the potential negative financial impact of the business problems?
- Discovered the buyers desired business outcomes, and are they achievable with you?
- Established with buyers a compelling reason to act or a compelling event?
- Agreed with buyers on the financial impact of delay or doing nothing?
- Uncovered or begun to help create an official budgeted project?
- Identified a successful reference site that is similar?

If you can honestly answer "Yes" to all the above questions, then you can start developing real business insight and discover what the key business problem is, how much it costs the company, and what impact it would have to remove the problem. If you cannot answer "Yes" to all the above questions, then you are at risk of applying your skills more in hope than reality. Remember, hope is not a good strategy! Decide now to progress the sale based on reality, not conjecture or driven by targets and managers. Applying this tool brings reality to your sale and value to your customer. Once this task is completed, then you need to check your data before you input to your CRM.

Opportunity Identification Qualification Metrics Tool

In Figure 5.4, there are three key steps to enable you to apply this tool and ensure that this is a genuine opportunity and one that you can win. This tool establishes the real financial impact of the problem your prospective customer is facing. In addition, and critically, it also answers the question for sales management: Do we know enough, and should we commit valuable demonstration and proposal resources to this opportunity?

GO TO THE TOOLBOX FOLDER AND OPEN 'QUALIFY: OPPORTUNITY METRICS'

Executive and Line of Business (LOB) Objectives (KPI's, SRO's)?	Business Problems? (List)	Business Pains linked to each Business Problem?	Potential Negative Financial Impact of each Business Pain?	Potential Positive Financial Impact of Solving the Business Pain	Potential Financial Impact of doing nothing?	Compelling reason/event to act?	What are our Unique Selling Points (USP's)?	What Technical Pain is each "Business Problem" linked to?	Desired Business Outcome (Linked to Business Problem)

Figure 5.4 Opportunity metrics tool. How to establish the real financial impact of the problem your prospective customer is facing. You must know and agree to the desired business outcome in financial terms

1. The most important factor for executive and line of business managers is identifying the financial impact of the identified problem. The salesperson can directly help by breaking the problem down into elements that we call business pain. In other words, it is not a real problem unless the impact is financial. That causes pain to the business. In this tool, the salesperson inputs the answers from the customer when they ask: What are the business pains linked to the problem stopping client meeting objectives? The answer goes in the business problem column. The next question is to ask: What are your desired business outcomes? The previous techniques described in this chapter will provide additional data for this column. Now you can complete the business outcome column.

2. Combined with your input to the questions what is the expected quantified financial impact amount in columns potential negative, potential positive, and impact of do nothing, then continue to input the answer in the compelling reason column to the question, what is driving your customer to act? Without an event or compelling reason, then there is no compelling reason to buy your solution. However, you may find that very often the prospective customer contact does not know the answer to these questions. This is good. It is the main reason for

applying this tool with your customer. It highlights what is not known so you can work together to establish and quantify these issues.

3. It is important you identify, communicate, and input the company product's unique value into unique selling points column. Combine this with inputting the technical reason causing business problem in technical pain column. You will use this data in the Discover Insights tool in the next chapter.

Case Study: The Barristers

Every Problem Really Is an Opportunity

I was coaching a sales team who were specifically working on a large, strategically important deal where the prospective customer was a partnership of top barristers in London. Their stated key problem, as identified by the senior partners and their chief technical officer (CTO), was that while their 112 barristers each had a laptop with software that enabled them to work anywhere in the world with key clients, the software was poor at connecting with the multiple varieties of connectivity and internet systems in different countries. As a result, the ability to connect between each other and their database in London was often compromised. They wanted much better connectivity software and technology to help them communicate and work more effectively.

The sales team had focused on how their company was a world leader with leading-edge technology, software, and support. They had multiple strong references from existing customers in the legal profession. The price quoted was competitive, and the software had been demonstrated successfully with the early stages of scoping and cost implementation almost completed. The team had feedback from the CTO that the senior partners were happy so far. However, they would not commit to signing the deal or agreeing to an implementation date.

The team and I spent a whole morning in an intense workshop where I questioned everything. Using the checklist techniques, we established that there were gaps in the qualification criterion. I concluded that the deal was never qualified correctly since there was no compelling business or financial reason to buy. The focus was on new technology. We had to go back to the very beginning and apply all the techniques and tools explained in this chapter. The key question that nobody could answer, including the potential customer, was: What the financial impact of each of the business problems and pains was due to the lack of good connectivity technology, and what was the financial impact of doing nothing? This is clearly shown in Figure 5.4 and is a key part of the qualification metrics tool.

I realize that, on reflection, it often seems a simple and obvious area to clarify, but sales organizations are often so proud of their world-leading technology, products, and services that they assume the technology is the focus. They create a business plan and return on investment document, highlighting how the technology will help resolve the technical problems, and so assume that this will remove the business problems. The key focus should always be on the financial impact of the problem on the customers key strategic business goals, including their personal key performance indicators. What does the customer really care about? In this case, what do the senior partners really care about? It turns out that when the senior partners were asked, they replied, "our key goal is always billing the client for every minute." A barrister's time is very expensive and runs into at least a few thousand per hour. For the sake of anonymity, I am simplifying things, but when we worked out on how much billing time was lost every time the barristers had a technical problem and could not communicate with the client due to those technical problems, it worked out at hundreds of thousands saved over a year if the technical issues were removed. That fact resonated with the senior partners, and the deal was signed very quickly when they realized billing revenue would increase and the cost of doing nothing was much higher than they realized.

CHAPTER 6

Business Insight

How to Gain Unique Business Insight

In Chapter 2, we identified the eight 'hard' skills and why they need to be improved to gain sales excellence. Discovering the customer's real problem and its impact on their business is probably the most important activity after the task of qualifying to make sure the opportunity is real. These skills are required today to filter your data to ensure accuracy before it goes into your Customer Relationship Management (CRM) and automation systems. In addition, at this stage in any sale, they provide the crucial ability and skills required to help the customer achieve their desired business outcomes and help you deliver real value for your customer. The result is increased sales revenue and desired productivity from the sales teams.

This chapter focuses on learning how to apply sales excellence discovery techniques and tools linked to practical exercises. The first and most important technique is to create insights into the business issues the customer is experiencing. Next, you need to know who the stakeholders are and know all of them. For example, who really influences the decision makers? You need to map them out and understand what the inter-relationships are between each. Knowing what, why, and how the issues affect their business requires what is called the directional questioning technique. Finally, we input that data into the insights tool to reveal your solution and how that will resolve the customer's issues.

This chapter ends with a focus on learning how to apply these unique sales excellence prospecting techniques and tools linked to practical exercises so that you can use them as filters or in parallel to integrate them into the CRM and sales process to ensure your data input is correct.

Business Insight and Stakeholder Discovery: Key Activities

- Have you delivered business insights and identified all key stakeholders?
- Are you aligned with buyers and decision makers?
- Do you fully understand the problems and possible solutions?

The most important principle is to align your activities with that of your buyer and stakeholders. In your discovery activities, you need to be aware that your potential customer has already developed their plan, identified and analyzed the impact of any blockages to stop them from achieving their key strategic business objectives (SBOs) in their plan, initiated a project to remove the blockages, and has now started to explore solutions from key vendors and suppliers. These potential blockages are what you should have discovered when you were first researching and prospecting for new business. Before you start asking the prospect lots of questions, it would be best that you know how to identify, qualify, and quantify the financial impact of the blockages on their business. Once this activity is completed, only then can you start investigating the problems, the impact of these problems, and discovering the possible solutions. The techniques and tools that follow will help you achieve that aim.

Buyer activities: Establishing vendor preference, exploring alternatives

Seller activities: Identify stakeholders, discover insight, create business value.

CRM stage: Qualified/recognizing/identifying solutions

SALES GOAL A: Establish vendor preference with key approvers, authorized signatories, and high influencers.

SALES GOAL B: Understand the full extent of the business problem. The impact on the organization is to complete requirements to achieve client-desired business outcomes to reach client business objectives and key performance indicators (KPIs).

Sales Goal A

It is important at this stage to identify all key decision makers, influencers, stakeholders in the company who will be involved in the buying and decision-making process. Then you must engage in activities that will build trust with those key decision makers and influencers. With your manager's help, the next step is to determine the resources that you and your team members require that will help progress and win the arguments with the identified key contacts. You must craft the right message(s) to the right ears by having peer-to-peer discussions. This means that you might need to ask your C-level executives to become involved in face-to-face calls with their counterparts. For example, the CTO of your company with the CTO of the prospects. If this does not happen, then issues will arise later in the sale, and it will be more difficult to progress to a decision. Relationships must be established now.

So, it is your task to identify all the key stakeholders' method of decision making and buying activity and involvement. By asking key questions to uncover each stakeholder's KPIs, SBOs, and personal risk/reward, you and your team and your executives will have a much better idea of what the personal compelling reason is to choose your solution and commit resources to buying and achieving a successful implementation. Once this task is completed, then you need to check your data before you input to your CRM.

Key Stakeholder Checklist: Sales Goal A

Ask yourself these critical questions. Have you:

- Identified all potential influencers, approvers, and decision makers?

- Assessed hierarchy and degree of influence/authority of each?
- Aligned business resources to key stakeholders?
- Crafted and delivered key messages to key stakeholders?
- Confirmed key influencers personal wins and which ones are blocked?
- Established strong peer-to-peer relationships and trust with key stakeholders?
- Identified buyers' internal sponsor/coach/mobilizer who prefers us?
- Identified competition and set tactical plans to neutralize?
- Identified who is coaching the competition inside the buyers' business?
- Identified your client's preference versus competition? Are you first, second, or third?

If you can honestly answer "Yes" to all the previous questions, then move on to discovering the real problems and issues using the techniques and tools in the next chapter. However, if you answered "No" to any of the questions, then you need to decide and create your strategy and influence map. What follows will help.

Hierarchy has been replaced by distributed teams. Who now has real buying power and influence? You must know and establish the following criterion:

- Name of the influencer.
- Describe their title.
- What is their value driver and business objective (Finance oriented? Operations?)
- Level of influence? High, medium, low.
- Are they a coach?
- Degree of preference?
- The level of contact with this person?
- Role—Approver, decision maker, recommender, sponsor?
- Alignment—Who manages the relationship?

HEIRARCHY IS GIVING WAY TO DISTRIBUTED TEAMS · Who has real buying power and influence?

INFLUENCE MAP CRITERIA

- Name of the Influencer;
- Describe their Title
- What is their value driver and business objective (Finance oriented? Operations?)
- Level of influence - High, medium, low
- Are they a coach?
- Degree of preference?
- The level of contact with this person?
- Role - Approver, Decision Maker, Recomender, Sponsor?
- Alignment - Who manages the relationship?

OBJECTIVES AND ACTIONS

| 1 | Decide influencer map criteria for the columns in Stakeholder Tool | 2 | Determine required relationships you need with each | 3 | Decide strategy and actions to influence the power buyers who influence approvers, decision makers, recommender, sponsors | 4 | Create strategy document and circulate to wider team |

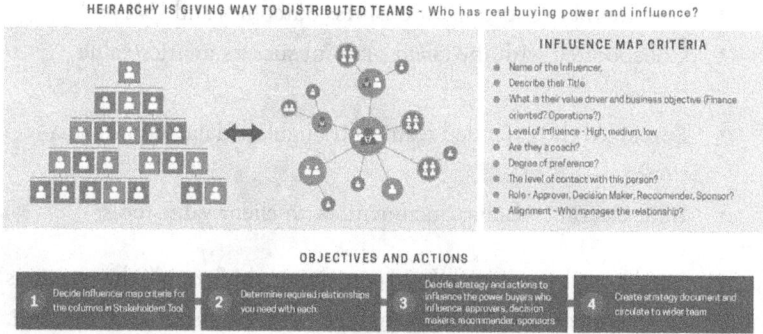

Figure 6.1 Influence map strategy and criteria. Identify and map out all key decision makers, influencers, stakeholders in the company that will be involved in the buying and decision-making process

Once you know the above facts, then it helps to make a simple drawing, placing each influencer in boxes, and showing the links between the key influencers. Always keep in mind these relationships. There is good software that exists to help complete this task for you.

To help you achieve this task, refer to Figure 6.1, where you must write down and create a diagram to draw out your conclusions and relationships within the company you are selling to. Answer the questions in the influence map criteria section. Write them down to help you understand what a complex relationship map might look like. Then once you have created this map, circulate it to your team to get their feedback and reassess and repeat regularly throughout the sales process.

Once the above task is completed, then you need to check your data before you input it to your CRM.

SALES GOAL B: The next step is probably one of the most important tasks that you must get right.

Business Insight/Value Discovering Activities Checklist

- Executed face-to-face interviews to gain client business insight?
- Confirmed business problems are blocking client business objectives?
- Discovered the client's criteria, definition, and vision of success?

- Confirmed clients desired business outcomes and vision?
- Collaborated with the client on joint success metrics/value drivers?
- Leveraged the extended team to triangulate data and information?
- Built customer-facing documents with client value tools?

If you can honestly answer "Yes, I am doing this" to all the previous questions, then you might have enough data to propose a solution. If you answered "No" to any the above questions, then perhaps the following discovery techniques might help:

- **Business insight**
- **Directional questioning**

In planning, we highlighted that knowing what to say when you get in front of C-level executives or key influencers is critical. That is why the technique of effective C-level questioning is in the beginning of the sales process. It is critical. For example, many senior executives would say the words spoken in a scene from the film *Wall Street* when the famous city stockbroker says to the young hopeful stockbroker trying to get a job in his company, "you were smart enough to get into my office to see me now tell me something I don't know." What the executive is demanding is for the young budding executive to have prepared a business insight that will genuinely help him and be of value. All top salespeople understand this point and always go into a sales call with unique business insights. Do you? If not then here is how to achieve that goal.

Business Insight

Now, in discovery, as we move into the very active part of any sale, the business insights technique in Figure 6.2 highlights the importance of creating value for the decision makers earlier in any sale. In the book *Insight Selling* by Schultz and Doerr, the authors highlight recent research, and taken from that data, they then divided selling into

5 STEPS TO CREATING REAL CLIENT VALUE

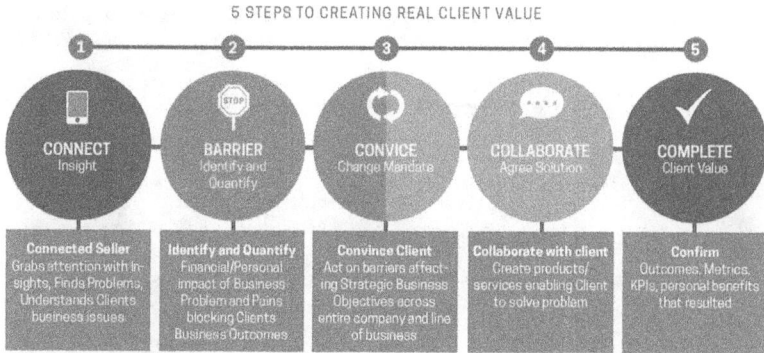

Figure 6.2 Business insights application. *A simple process applying creative insights into the business issues the customer is experiencing, which will start to deliver real value*

three parts: connect, convince, and collaborate. I have added two more stages.

Most competent sellers can "connect" with their prospective customer. However, without an "insight" to grab attention, this can be difficult, especially for inexperienced sellers. In fact, to overcome this issue, many companies are using presales and tele-sales called inside sales and third-party companies to do this sales task for the main sellers. This can be a good strategy, but often the resulting hot lead is not qualified, nor is the value of providing a potential solution to the clients' business problem quantified at this stage. Salespeople tend to move to "convince" too fast, and this causes resistance and objections and stops progress. It is critically important to identify and quantify the financial impact of the problems and business issues. We covered this a little in the previous "qualify" stage, but it is now imperative. Once this is revealed and the client agrees, you can then move on. If this is not done at this stage, then it will cause a major "barrier" to your sale and produce major objections to the sale later, usually at the negotiation stage. "Collaboration" is significantly improved when you can link your business insights to your solution and prove it will help achieve the customers SBOs.

ARE YOUR CLIENTS BUSINESS OBJECTIVES ACHIEVED WITH YOUR SOLUTION?

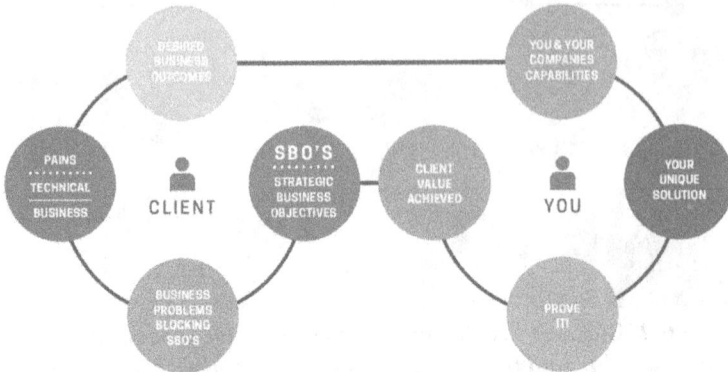

Figure 6.3 Achieving business value. Value is only achieved when your company's capabilities deliver the desired business outcomes and meet the strategic business objectives

Business Value Only Achieved by Meeting Strategic Business Objectives

Are your prospective customer's strategic business and personal objectives achieved with your capabilities and solution? Real customer/client value is only achieved when your company's capabilities combine with your proven solution to meet and achieve your customer's strategic and personal business objectives by removing the business and technical blocks to those objectives to result in meeting the desired business outcomes in financial terms. Figure 6.3 highlights the parallel path required for you to meet your customer's needs.

Directional Questioning—The Key to Discovering the Impact of the Business Problem

You need to link your company's capabilities and solutions to the potential customer's desired business outcomes. In addition, it is critical to ask "high-yield questions" before you propose or demonstrate your solution or product. This technique is called directional questioning. You must find and quantify the financial pain or indeed financial benefits of resolving the business issue and its impact, positive or negative, on the client.

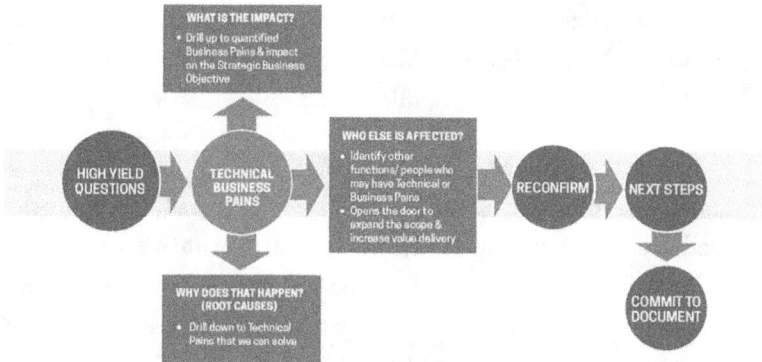

Figure 6.4 Directional questioning. What, why, and how do the technical and business issues impact, and who is affected most, when documented will help reveal the issues

In Figure 6.4, the model reflects that most social psychology research, for example, from Robert B. Cialdini in his book *Influence: The Psychology of Persuasion*, agrees that there are seven key categories of high-yield questions. The answers will help discover what really matters to the customer, and that knowledge is critical in applying the art of persuasion. I have listed them in easy-to-use language attached to each category:

1. Business objectives: What are you trying to do? What is your strategic objective or your business need requiring a solution?
2. Business pain: Why can't you do it today? What business barrier would you face in trying to achieve your objective?
3. Technical pain: Why can't you do it today? What technical issues would you face in trying to achieve your objective?
4. Desired outcome: What does success look like to you? What would be your ideal desired business outcome?
5. Stakeholders: Who cares about this most? Who decides, and who are the key influencers? Who is most impacted by the impact of the business pain?
6. Risk: What are the consequences and financial impact if nothing is done? What are your stakeholders concerns about risk?

7. Metric value drivers: What metric can you measure to determine success for this objective? What is the financial impact of the business improvement in this metric?

It is worth memorizing these questions and be able to ask them naturally in a sales call. Reconfirm the answers verbally and in writing and make sure you agree on the next steps with the prospective customer before you move on. If you do not write it down, agree, and document the answers, then it will trip you up later, probably when you are negotiating the final terms and conditions.

Business Insight/Value Tool Checklist Sales Goal B

Ask yourself these critical questions. Have you:

- Captured in writing the client's business problems that link to technical problems?
- Captured SBOs, value drivers, and KPIs?
- Confirmed and agreed with the client on the desired business outcome and success metrics?
- Gained agreement with the client that your solution capabilities can remove their business problems?
- Identified the compelling event or compelling reason to act and client agrees?
- Established the go-live and latest order date, and the client agrees?
- Understood fully the decision making and buying process?
- Completed a competitive analysis, strategy, and tactics plan agreed upon with the manager?

If you can honestly answer "Yes" to all the above questions, then you might have enough data to propose a solution. If you cannot answer "Yes" to all the above questions, then you must gain more data to help establish a solution that you can propose that will remove the problems and blocks to the customer issues. I suggest this tool will transform that process.

GO TO THE TOOLBOX FOLDER AND OPEN 'DISCOVER: INSIGHTS'					
DISCOVERY					
What business insights can you provide and what value does the client want? (Capture stakeholders vision, goals and compelling reason to act)					
Objective	Current Barriers		Desired Outcome	Stakeholder	Risk	Metric Value Driver
What are you trying to do? What is the need and /or objective?	Business Pain - Why can't you do it today? What issues/challenges do you face that blocks achieving the objective?	Technical Pain - Why can't you do it today? What issues/challenges do you face that blocks achieving the objective?	What does success look like to you? What is the capability desired?	Who cares about this most? Who are the key influencers? Who is most impacted by it?	What are the consequences and impact if nothing is done? What are stakeholders concerns about risk?	What metric can you measure to determine success for this objective? What is the financial impact of the business improvement in this metric?
trying to get rid of unpredictability	duy cannot reach revenue goals	lacking in store capacity	expanding system	CTO		
	unpredicable area of the vision	sytem outages	no outages	CIO		

Figure 6.5 Insights tool

Discovering Business Insight/Value Tool

The technique recommended to apply this tool correctly is to work directly with the key contacts in your prospective customer and share the tool and the results. It is a customer-facing tool, so work directly with the key stakeholders using your laptop. By asking the five highlighted questions and completing the columns, this tool contains the customer's desired outcomes in their own words. The tool produces a value ladder, which becomes a shorthand version and easy summary that can be applied to the main business case document for the return on investment that you will eventually produce for the customer.

There are additional questions that make up the seven customer-facing questions the customer must input into the insights tool so that together you gain insight into what the customer really values. These are shown in Figure 6.5 and will help the tool automatically produce a value ladder that will help the customer as much as you to determine the valued solution.

Add the above questions to the complete list of columns and questions in the tool, and it will guide your discovery questions. Importantly, by inputting the answers into the tool, you can share the results with your customer, who will see their own answers, which

Objectives	What are you trying to do? (What is the objective / need?)
Business Pains	Why can't you do it today? (What business barrier would you face in trying to achieve objective?)
Technical Pains	Why can't you do it today? (What technical issues would you face in trying to achieve objective?)
Desired Outcome	What does success look like to you? (What would be an ideal desired business outcome?)
Stakeholder	Who cares about this most? (Who are the key influencers? Who is most impacted by the pain?)
Risk	What are the consequences and impact if nothing is done? (What are stakeholders concerns about risk?)
Metric Value Driver	What metric can you measure to determine success for this objective? (What is the financial impact of the business improvement in this metric?)

Figure 6.6 The seven customer value questions

they can then regularly amend and update. The tool will become a real support method for the customer to make decisions.

There are two sections in the insights tool, as shown in Figure 6.6

Discovery Goal

- What does the client want?
- What are the stakeholder's visions, goals, compelling reasons to act?

Columns to Be Completed

- Objectives, current barriers, desired outcomes, stakeholders, risk, metric value driver.

Solution and Proof Goal

- What solution do we propose?
- Can we enable decision makers to understand how and where the solution creates value?

What does the client want?

What are the stakeholder's visions, goals, compelling reasons to act?

Objectives, current barriers, desired outcomes, stakeholders, risk, metric value driver.

What solution do we propose?

Can we enable decision makers to understand how and where the solution creates value?

Columns to Be Completed

Solution, client value proposition, client agreement.

In many companies today, they use AI and sales process systems to enable what is called discovery. However, often the customer is left out of the direct process. In addition, they are increasingly averse to answering questions that the sales organization should know anyway, and the customer does not know how the answers are ultimately being used. Recent retail and business research highlights that many customers find the constant surveys and discovery questions carried out today not only irritating but also of no value at all to their day-to-day lives and business objectives. What is unique about this tool is that when applied correctly with face-to-face customer direct input, it will then contain the customer's real business answers to describe their current business problems, desired solutions, and outcomes, and not the salesperson's wishful thinking answers. The resulting proposal and business cases produced will contain answers that they will recognize as their direct statements. In short, it will contain accurate data to then inform your CRM and AI questions.

Case Study: The Insurance Company

How the Business Insights Tool Became Invaluable to the Potential Customer

When you look at Figures 6.5 and 6.6, you can see very specific questions being asked. However, the key to the success of the tool is that it is what I call a customer-facing tool. My recommendation is that when you get in front of the potential customer, either virtually or face-to-face, turn the tool toward the stakeholder, show and share the questions directly with them, and, if you have a good relationship, ask them to input the answers. The key to this tool is the answers are in the stakeholder's own words, not your interpretation of their answers to your questions. You can use this tool, and the data produced, later in the sale. The critical element is that the stakeholder feels personally engaged, involved, and valued. For example, in this example, the main contact was the chief financial officer (CFO). When the tool asked him, what are you trying to do? He answered, I need insight into our rebate position. I want to reduce labor overheads associated with rebates. I need to accurately manage the rebate position. Then the tool asked multiple questions linked to those primary needs as shown in Figure 6.6. Each answer was an input by the CFO into the tool but was limited to a few sentences, so he had to really think about his answers. He answered the rest of the questions regarding the business and technical reasons why he could not do it today, what did success look like to him, who else cared about these issues, what are the consequences of doing nothing, and how is he going to measure the success. Then the tool created a graphic showing his objectives, his business drivers, his technical pains, and his desired outcomes. We then completed our section, which highlights our solution and capability to each of his needs. The tool produced another graphic with our capability shown. We then had what is called a value ladder. The CFO immediately saw his own words answered in a simple but powerful graphic.

In addition, we now knew all the other stakeholders involved. We asked permission from the CFO to meet each one of them and complete tool with them. This was completed, and the answers from all the stakeholders were put straight into our demonstration of our solution and our proposal. When it came to the presentation to all the stakeholders, they each recognized their answers, and more importantly, our solution was laser-focused on their needs and not our interpretation. We won the deal very quickly. Interestingly, the CFO asked our permission to use the tool internally with his staff because it helped them analyze, simplify, and communicate their complex issues.

The additional value of this tool is when your relationship is poor or all you have is an RFP (request for pricing or proposal), you can use the tool to answer the questions yourself and check if you really understand the issues and how your solution adds value by resolving the issues that matter to the prospective customer. I suggest you share this with your key contact. You may find this breaks the barriers, and you start a meaningful collaboration.

See for yourself. Go to the Appendix and complete the exercise.

CHAPTER 7

Business Proposals

How to Gain Business Outcomes

In Chapter 2, we identified the eight 'hard' skills and why they need to be improved to gain sales excellence. Discovering the customer's real problem and its impact on their business has been achieved, and now we move to proposing our solution. However, since selling is not a straight-line process, the customer may already have demanded a proposal, or you are responding to an RFP, which is a request for pricing. A great book on this topic is *RFPs Suck!* by Tom Searcy. If possible, do not respond with a pricing proposal immediately. It is quite feasible and reasonable to point out to the customer you will be more valuable to them and present a much better proposal and pricing structure if you knew just a little bit more about their problem, issues, and possible expected solutions. If they accept your suggestion, go back to qualification and discovery techniques and tools.

However, if the customer insists on a completed RFP and proposal, then this chapter focuses on learning how to apply sales excellence proposal techniques and tools linked to practical exercises. The first and most important technique is to apply the checklist and make sure you have covered all the basic requirements. Next, you need to complete a proposal template and be confident you can present your proposal effectively either virtually or face-to-face. Finally, we input all the data from our process so far and apply the winning solution tool to present your solution and how that will resolve the customer's issues with a Return On Investment (ROI) document if possible.

This chapter ends with a focus on learning how to apply the unique sales excellence proposing techniques and tools. These are linked to practical exercises to ensure your progressing the sale activities and final negotiation steps are effective in winning the sale.

The most important principle is to align your activities with that of your buyer and stakeholders. In your proposed activities, you need to be aware that your potential customer has already developed their plan, identified and analyzed the impact of any blockages that stop them from achieving their key strategic business objectives in their plan, initiated a project to remove the blockages, started to explore solutions from key vendors and suppliers, and is now evaluating your competitor's proposals and solutions. Before you start making proposals and demonstrating your solutions, it would be best that you know how to identify, qualify, and quantify the financial impact of the blockages on their business. You must discover what the real value to them is when the blockages are removed. Finally, you must demonstrate convincingly how and why your solution will transform their business. Once this activity is completed, only then can you start presenting possible solutions. The techniques and tools that follow will help you achieve that aim.

Business Outcome Proposing: Key Activities

Buyer activities: Evaluate proposals, vendor solutions, and alternatives.

Seller activities: Propose solution and quantify business outcomes

CRM stage: Qualified/gaining agreement

SALES GOAL: Define and present a solution that meets the agreed "business objectives," delivers desired "business outcomes," and confirms "business value" and unique capabilities of your solution to the client that outperforms the competitors alternatives being evaluated.

These skills are required today to filter your data to ensure accuracy before it goes into your Customer Relationship Management (CRM) and automation systems. In addition, they provide the crucial abilities and skills required to achieve the desired business outcomes and deliver real value for your customer and sales revenue and desired productivity from the sales teams.

Propose Value: Business Outcomes

- Do you know that real value in customer terms truly exists?
- Are you aligned with your buyer?
- Are you personally adding value?

Business Outcomes Proposing Activities Checklist

- Define and document your unique solution and capabilities.
- Highlight your unique capabilities to solve technical pains and business problems.
- Remove linked business pains to achieve client business outcomes/objectives.
- Document this business value and quantify business outcome to prove client ROI.
- Completed team presentations, implementation plans to client and sponsors.
- Document, gain agreement on Proof Of Concept /Proof Of Technology (POC/POT) criteria, timeline, and outcomes.
- Document, gain agreement on workshop and business outcomes criteria.

If you can honestly answer "Yes I am doing this" to all the above activities, then you can start actively progressing the sale, committing your wider resources, and engaging additional resources. If you cannot answer "Yes" to all the above questions then perhaps these techniques might help.

- **Proposal checklist**
- **Proposal template**
- **Presentation planning**

Proposal Checklist

Before you put together any proposal, there are four key areas you need to check you have achieved. This checklist is intended to help you identify what is missing and the actions to be taken to fill the gaps.

1. **Understand the client's needs and confirm the compelling reason to act.**

When it comes to proposing a solution or product, the salesperson often feels comfortable they have identified the main reason the prospect wants to invest in their product or service. For example, the support contract will run out soon, or the prices will rise, or, even better, they want to reduce costs by using a financial package software to consolidate the multiple company accounts across the globe. However, it turns out that the reason most companies purchase new products, or a new service, is that the local or department purchase is linked to and dependent upon a companywide strategic business initiative. You must ask that question, and if this is found to be the case, then it is critical to link your solution to that strategic objective by showing how it will help achieve that company objective. Many sales can be progressed more quickly when you link to a companywide objective or project. For example, after the COVID global epidemic, a large retailer had launched a major reconstruction of their retail shops and online services across the world. I was coaching a UK team of a large IT services company, who were trying to close a deal selling financial planning software to this retailer. The deal was progressing very slowly with lots of objections and stop/starts. I encouraged the team to ask the questions: Was this local country software purchase linked to any strategic business objective? Are there specific problems and needs driving this purchase? Finally, were there any unique new capabilities that needed to be built in? The answer was yes, and it was discovered that the financial planning software that the UK retailer team was buying was crucial to the overall success of the global project, as it was to be used as a test site, and if successful, it was going to be replicated internationally. Having asked the question and discovered the global project, the UK IT services team shared the opportunity with the global team. The sale went from being a local country deal to a global deal. It was demonstrated to the global executives how each country subsidiary could easily co-ordinate and consolidate the software. The executive board agreed on a global deal, and in each country, a local deal was struck that was many times the value of the initial local UK team's deal. Everyone was a winner.

2. **Develop the client's perception of our unique value with our solution.**

Often my answer to the statement from sellers that their solution is unique is, why? The answers usually reflect the company's unique selling points (USP), which are only in the mind of the seller and not at all in the mind of the buyer, who is looking at all the vendors. In addition, the USP is proven to be worthless to the buyer who does not perceive it unique or valuable. The urge to win has blinded the seller to the fact that perhaps there is no USP. The tactic here is to absolutely establish and demonstrate USPs that are genuinely unique and of real business value. Self-delusion is common in the human mind.

3. **Confirm the client's expected benefit and value proposition.**

In any murder mystery story, the detective must reveal and produce convincing evidence that reflects the facts of the case and proves conclusively whodunit! It is the same principle when making a sales proposition. Look at the questions in the third section of Figure 7.1. If you cannot produce evidence, then your proposal will be weak and will not succeed. You must gain that evidence as you progress through your sale. The techniques and tools in this book will help immensely.

4. **Confirm that the client's delivery expectations are being met.**

It is a common refrain in today's world of business that the plan was good, but the execution of that plan was terrible. In the retail Business to Consumer (B2C) environment, the result is you lose individual customers. The result is an unhappy customer and bad publicity internally and externally on social media, for example. The result in the Business to Business (B2B) business world of not meeting expectations is that it can destroy your company. You must answer "yes" to all the

UNDERSTAND THE CLIENT NEEDS AND CONFIRM THE COMPELLING REASON TO ACT
What strategic business initiative is this action tied to?
What needs/ issues/ problems are driving it?
What new capabilities are desired by the client?
DEVELOP THE CLIENT'S PERCEPTION OF OUR UNIQUE VALUE WITH OUR SOLUTION
What capabilities differentiate us from the competition? What is this worth to the client?
What is the client's perception of our unique Value?
How much do we need to Win?
CONFIRM THE CLIENT'S EXPECTED BENEFIT AND VALUE PROPOSITION
What do we propose to deliver on this client's desired business capabilities and expectations?
What is the value proposition? What is the compelling business case?
What shows that we have the support of the key decision leaders?
What would be required for Client to become a client reference?
CONFIRM THE CLIENT'S DELIVERY EXPECTATION'S ARE BEING MET
Do we know the service level and logistics expected and agreed to?
Can we meet both our own and the Client's financial targets?
Are we delivering what the client is expecting and what we have contracted to do?
How will this delivery impact client satisfaction/expectations?

Figure 7.1 Proposal checklist

questions in the fourth section of Figure 7.1, and we have a plan to reduce the impact of poor delivery and can alleviate any consequences.

Proposal Template

Unfortunately, most of the available online sales research from websites such as GrowthHub reveals that many proposals do not come close to matching the expectations of the proposed customer. It would take another book to detail exactly what is required and how to achieve a good proposal and build a team with the skill set to write and present excellent proposals. Too often it is left to the sales team, who often do not possess the skills to write and present professional proposals. Many companies now have a separate team to achieve this task, and some use my tools to filter the data going into the proposal. For example, a group sales director of the five sales teams I was coaching decided to add my qualification opportunity tool as a filter and instructed the proposal team that if any proposal from a salesperson did not pass the qualification criteria in the tool, then he would not commit to financing the writing and preparing of the proposal, as it was very costly to produce and then lose the sale. This resulted in fewer proposals and reduced costs but significantly increased the win rate from 1:4 to 1:3 with resulting a 30 percent uplift in sales revenue. A good result. However, using the content and following the principles outlined in the template in Figure

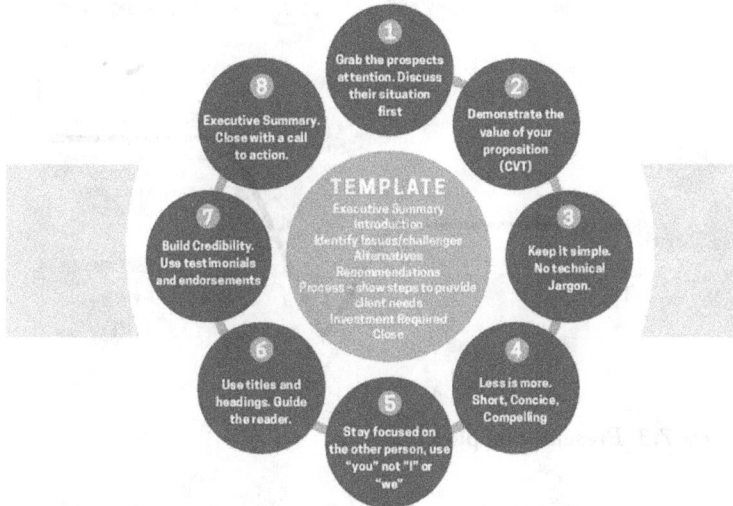

Figure 7.2 Proposal template

7.2 would be a good start to achieve increasing the effectiveness and professionalism of any sales proposal.

Presentation Planning

The presentation planning graphic (Figure 7.3) is called the heartbeat because it looks like a sinus rhythm of a human heart. It starts from a regular plateau, then a strong upbeat to pump up the blood, then a drop in activity, then a plateau, then another strong upbeat, and so on. Your presentation should be similar in activity. Start strong, then give the detail, followed by another upbeat strong statement, then more detail, and so on until the final finish with a strong upbeat message.

The content of the presentation to executives and management should follow the sales process pattern we described in Chapter 2. It is so important that I repeat the formula again to remind you to use it during presentations and proposals.

- GRAB customer prospect attention by showing INSIGHT to key business problems

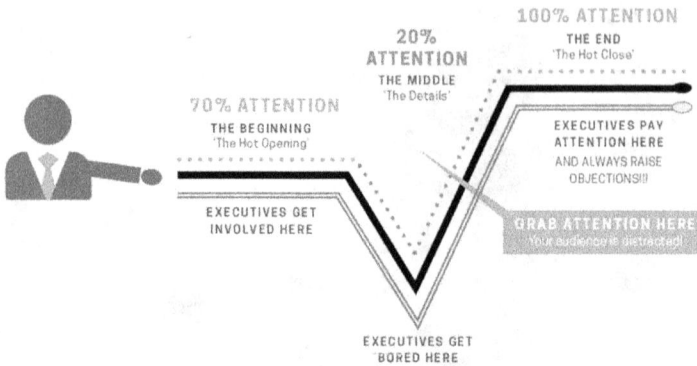

Figure 7.3 Presentation planning

- INDENTIFY problems that BLOCK their key STRATEGIC BUSINESS OBJECTIVES
- QUANTIFY IMPACT of the BUSINESS PAINS caused by business problems
- SEPARATE their TECHNICAL PAINS and LINK each to specific BUSINESS PAINS
- HIGHLIGHT YOUR UNIQUE CAPABILITY to solve TECHNICAL PAINS to then remove linked BUSINESS PAINS and to achieve BUSINESS OUTCOMES and OBJEC-TIVES
- NOW PROVE IT WITH YOUR UNIQUE SOLUTION
- CUSTOMER UNIQUE VALUE is achieved

Having created content and data by applying the proposal's techniques, it is now time to create your proposal. The following checklist tool is critical. Any missing parts in your business proposal gained from the summary of your efforts so far will trip you up when you get to the negotiation stages. Objections to the sale will become clear and you may well lose your very visible forecasted sale or at the very least the deal slips into the next quarter or year, which you will then have to justify to your management.

Business Outcomes Proposing Tool Checklist

Ask yourself these critical questions. Have you:

- Quantified the business outcomes and business results your solution delivers?
- Demonstrated your unique capabilities and value that differentiates your solution?
- Stakeholders have agreed proposed solution uniquely solves their business problem?
- Quantified the alternative of doing nothing and articulated this to our client?
- Proven that client has demonstrated agreement with us? For example, joint presentation?
- Key decision makers confirmed that the solution provides compelling ROI, reason to act?
- Key decision makers agree that the proposal achieves desired business outcomes?
- Documented and shared with approvers/decision makers that solution achieves ROI?

If you can honestly answer "Yes" to all the above questions, then your proposal is good and you can start actively progressing the sale, committing your wider resources, and engaging additional resources to drive on to win the sale in the forecasted time.

If you cannot answer "Yes" to all the above questions, then go back to previous steps, especially qualification and discovery, and redo the proposal. It is that simple. Unless you have achieved the above steps, do not create and deliver a proposal and do not move on to progressing your sale however attractive that option looks. You must go back and ask, how and why you got involved in this opportunity? My suggestion is always start by reapplying the qualification opportunity metrics tool.

Unfortunately, in today's pressurized sales world, too many sales organizations respond, almost automatically, to a request for pricing and/or proposal. The correct and more successful response is to respond by saying you will provide an RFP, but first, you need to meet up to understand more about their business. This approach requires discipline and management approval. It requires competent qualification and discovery methods that allow for the fact that the customer has already researched what they need on the internet and chosen at least three vendors before approaching you and them. The good news is that you have received an RFP. Hopefully, you have learned to go back and fill in all your gaps in knowledge. Now you have created a powerful proposal, presented your solution, and are confident that you are delivering value. How do you now progress to negotiate a final sale and successful implementation? The next chapters answer that question. But first, a real example presenting a proposal.

Case Study: Motor Corporation

How the Owl Won the Senior Executives Confidence

We were due to present to a global leader in the motor industry. It was the culmination of months of work. All the key executives were going to be present many of whom we had not met. We had applied all the techniques contained in this chapter. I am using this example to highlight it is important to have a relationship or personal insight for all the executives including the ones you have not met. The reason is, you need to grab attention, as shown in Figure 7.3, right from the start when the executives are paying attention to enable engagement and be connected when you present and are explaining concepts to key people. The key components of explanation are contained in Ros Atkins excellent book, *The Art of Explanation.*

I was involved as the international coach. I suggested that we each be allocated an executive and find out as much as we can about them and work out how to incorporate that information in our presentation. I had the CEO as my target. I discovered he was an avid ornithologist or bird watcher. His dream was to see a snowy owl in its natural wild habitat. There was only one place in the United Kingdom where you could do that, and it is in the Shetland Isles. As it happened, I had been to Shetland as a student and experienced the joy of seeing a snowy white owl in the wild. We all found out something about each executive in a similar vein and incorporated it in an innovative and original way into our presentation. The approach was stunningly successful, and we held their attention throughout. It may seem such a small matter, but our approach not only differentiated us from the competition it also showed that we cared about what they cared about. In today's business world, that is increasingly very important. We won the deal.

CHAPTER 8

Proof and Progress

How to Gain Proof of Outcomes

In Chapter 2, we identified the eight 'hard' skills and why they need to be improved to gain sales excellence. The hard skill of progressing the sale and gaining proof and agreement of the customer's desired business outcomes by collaborating with the customer team to solve their business problems and their financial impact on their business will now be the critical activity. Get this right and you will win the sale. However, it is at this point in any sale that everything can come to a halt, and activity from and with the customer stops. That is an obvious sign that all is not well. It may be a good sign, but it is critical to know the real status of your sale.

This chapter focuses on a unique methodology that you can learn quickly, which applies sales excellence progressing techniques that provide input data into a powerful scorecard system tool that will deliver actionable insights that you can execute and measure to progress your sale to a successful recorded conclusion. It also provides sales management with a powerful deal review and cadence system.

The most important principle is to align your activities with that of your buyers and stakeholders. In your progression of sale activities, you need to be aware that your potential customer has:

- Already developed their plan;
- Identified and analyzed the impact of any blockages that stop them from achieving their key strategic business objectives in their plan;
- Initiated a project to remove the blockages;
- Started to explore solutions from key vendors and suppliers;

- Has evaluated your competitor's proposals and solutions;
- Now wants to prove the technology and the concept of the proposed solution.

Before you agree or start a proof of concept of your solution, it would be best that you have identified, qualified, and quantified the financial impact of the blockages on their business, discovered what the real value is to them for the blockages to be removed, and demonstrated convincingly how and why your solution will transform their business. Once these activities are completed and you are aligned with the buying process, only then can you start carrying out proof-of-concept workshops and activities. The techniques and tools that follow will help you achieve that aim.

Proving and Progressing: Key Activities

Buyer activities: Prove the technology and validate the proposed business outcomes.

Seller activities: Prove the quantified business outcomes. Align and agree on joint actions.

CRM stage: Conditionally agreed.

SALES GOAL: Gained acceptance and agreement from the client on the exact solution set, financial investment, and implementation resources required.

To repeat my mantra throughout this book, the skills required today need to be good enough to ensure you filter your data to deliver accuracy before it goes into your Customer Relationship Management (CRM) and automation systems that produce sales forecasts. You need the crucial ability and skills to always achieve the desired business outcomes and deliver real value for your customer. This approach will produce the planned sales revenue and desired productivity from the sales teams.

We will now focus on learning how to apply these unique sales excellence sales progression techniques and tools, highlight a successful case history, download the techniques and tools from the Appendix, and practice them, including how to integrate the data produced into your CRM and sales automation processes.

Progress Solution: Proving and Progressing Techniques

- Is your solution compelling and convincing?
- Are you aligned with your buyer?

Proving and Progressing Activities Checklist

- Post solution business outcomes implementation success metrics.
- Proof of concept/technology outcomes and expectations.
- Business value and return on investment (ROI) agreed and proposed.
- Formal solution proposal presented with implementation details.
- Decision and purchasing process methods
- Compelling event or reason to act identified
- Date of purchase order

If you can honestly answer "Yes I am doing this" to all the above activities, then you can start actively progressing the sale, committing your wider resources, and engaging additional resources. If you cannot answer "Yes" to all the above questions, then perhaps the following techniques might help:

- **Sales review clinics**
- **Progress actions**
- **Team selling**

Sales Review Clinics

Pulling all the team together to meet regularly in a structured environment is a key tactic in progressing any sale and highlighting any last-minute issues that have been missed. The first step is to make sure that your CRM is up-to-date. You invite everyone involved in the sale. Technical, support, personnel, admin, presales, finance, legal, and all salespeople, including the managers. Figure 8.1 summarizes the process.

WEEK 1 — FORECASTED DEALS UPDATED AND IN CRM
Deals are updated and segmented based on revenue size, industry, solution type, margin.

WEEK 2 — DEAL SELECTING & SCHEDULING
Seller sends selected Deals to trained Facilitator using Template. Facilitator and seller schedule date and Facilitator sends invites to attendees on Template.

WEEK 3 — DEAL PREP SELLER PRE WORK
Sales Opportunity Metrics, Insights and Stakeholder Tools are completed and provided to Facilitator by seller. Facilitator works with the seller and manager to ensure resources and participants.

WEEK 4 - DEAL CLINICS HELD

WEEK 4 — DEAL ACTION PLAN
Facilitator applies The Five Pillars of Actions: documents action items using sales tools output and data. actions and status are rolled up to all department managers and operations teams to execute actions.

ON-GOING ON DEMAND — DEAL AND OPPORTUNITY PROGRESSION
Facilitator establishes check point meetings to ensure deal progression is being achieved. Seller reviews actions with manager and updates Sales Tools.

ON-GOING ON DEMAND — DEAL REPORTING
Facilitator decides completion status with manager and seller. Weekly, Quarterly dynamic reporting.
* Win/Loss
* Progression
* Regression

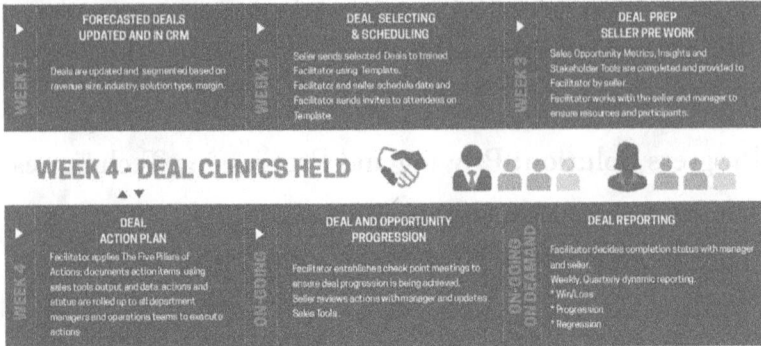

Figure 8.1 Sales review clinics

A facilitator (not the sales manager) is appointed who chairs the deal review meeting and guides the participants. The facilitator follows "the five pillars" approach detailed in the next technique section entitled Progress Actions.

Week 1: Forecasted Deals Updated and in CRM

Deals are updated and segmented based on revenue size, industry, solution type, margin.

Week 2: Deal Selecting and Scheduling

Seller sends selected deals to the trained facilitator using the deal opportunity template.

Facilitator and seller schedule Deal Clinic (DC) date and facilitator sends invites to attendees on the template. Figure 8.2 is a good example of a template summarizing the critical information.

Week 3: Deal Prep and Seller Pre Work

Sales opportunity metrics, insights, and stakeholder tools are completed and provided to facilitator by seller for DC. Facilitator works with the seller and manager to ensure resources and participants.

Name :	Opportunity/Cust Name:	Forecasted:	Rev/Margin:
Topic	**Summary status**		
Customer Problem to Solve			
Key Decision Makers and the status of relationship			
Proposed Solution			
Compelling Reason to Act / Timing of Deal			
Key technical influencers and their product biases			
Historical Account Activity or other factors that would affect this opportunity			
Primary Competitors			
Project Funding Status			

Figure 8.2 Deal opportunity template

Week 4: Deal Action Plan

Facilitator applies "the five pillars" of actions and documents action items from DC using sales tools output and data. DC actions and status are rolled up to all department managers and operations teams to execute actions.

On-Going Activity: Deal and Opportunity Progression

Facilitator establishes checkpoint meetings to ensure that deal progression is being achieved. Seller reviews actions with manager and updates sales tools.

On-Going and On-Demand Activity: Deal Reporting

Facilitator decides completion status with manager and seller.
     Weekly and quarterly dynamic reporting.

THE FIVE PILLARS OF ACTIONS

CLIENT RELATIONSHIPS	VALUE PROPOSITION	TECHNICAL	COMMERCIAL	COMPETITION
• If purchase order (PO) was to be signed tomorrow, who would sign the internal PO process and who signs the PO for external suppliers/vendors? • Do we have a relationship with all these stakeholders? Review key clients and their relationships. • Decide who on our team is most focused on each client Line of Business leader? • What actions are required to ensure these relationships are strong?	• What problem are we helping the client solve? • Why is it compelling? Why does the client care? • Is this a strategic or tactical problem for the client? • What actions are in place to determine the "real" problem the client is willing to spend money on? • If the problem is well defined, what actions are required to determine the right solution? • What actions are required to show the value of the solution to the key stakeholders?	• What is the technical environment? • Who are the key influencers and what are their biases? • Pro our company or Anti our company? • What actions are in place to deal with the anti company biases? • What actions are in place to create technical excitement? What actions will inspire the client tech team? For example, can we make them feel like our technology will make their lives easier? • If a Proof of Concept is required, what actions are in place to ensure the scope is to our advantage?	• Does the client have money and willingness to spend? • What are the client processes that must be handled to get to signature, approvals, commitment, P.O.? • What actions are in place to move the deal through the client internal processes? • What actions are in place to provide the client with information, documentation, stats, business case data? • What actions are in place to handle common negotiation tactics used by the client?	• Who is the primary competition? What is their relationship with the client? Are they going after the same problem? • What tactics will they use, technically and commercially? • What actions will create fear uncertainty and doubt (FUD) for the competitors solution, technology and commercial viability? • What actions are in place to avoid bake-off style comparisons? • What actions are in place to frame the discussion to our advantage? • What actions are in place to handle the commercial strategies?

Figure 8.3 Progress actions: the five pillars

Highlights in CRM Report

- ○ Win/loss
- ○ Progression
- ○ Regression

Progress Actions: The Five Pillars

Progressing your sale after you have proposed a solution is probably the most important task a salesperson has to achieve. This is where most sales become stuck. Over the years of coaching and research, I have developed what I call "the five pillars" of sales progression. Figure 8.3 graphically demonstrates a summary of the approach, but it may help to clarify the detail and how it works in practice. In any successful deal progression, there are five key areas that help define actions for tactical sales progression. I call these "the five pillars" of the sale.

The five pillars are:

1. The client relationship.
2. The value proposition and the problem to solve.
3. The current technical environment.
4. The commercial realities.
5. The primary competition.

1. The client relationships

Review your key clients, their relationships, and who on the team is most focused on each one, including the executive sponsor, budget holders, project owner, business users, key influencers, purchasing, technical staff, and so on. Ask the team who has a strong relationship with the authorized decision maker or makers, that is, the people signing the order. Do you know who signs the purchase order, internally by executives and externally to suppliers? There are usually at least three authorized personnel. Write down what actions are required to ensure these relationships are strong and are peer-to-peer. For example, a CFO, who signs purchase orders, often prefers to talk with a peer. Ask your own CFO to contact the prospective customer's CFO and arrange a face-to-face or virtual meeting. This always smooths the path to getting an order.

2. The value proposition and the problem to solve.

The team leader must ask what problem we are solving for the client and why it is compelling. Why does the client care, and is this a strategic or tactical problem for the client? The team must decide and write down what actions are in place to determine the real problem the client is willing to spend money on and will move to buy the solution.

The team leader must ensure the problem is well defined, decide what actions are required to determine the right solution, and arrange workshops to work to resolve these issues.

Finally, you must prove the relevant value, so the team needs to agree the specific actions required to show the value of the solution to the key stakeholders.

3. The current technical environment.

The team leader asks the technical team: What is the lay of the land? Who are the key technical influencers, and what are their biases? Are they pro or anti our solution and company branding? It is important to detail the current technical environment and agree on that document with the prospect's technical team.

At this stage, the team needs to put in place actions to combat any bias against the solution being proposed. These fears in the client are usually driven by the competition.

The next step is to put actions in place to create technical excitement. This is best achieved by running a proof of technology workshop. Decide before the workshop which actions will inspire the client tech team. Make them feel your technology will make their lives easier.

4. The commercial realities

It may seem an obvious question, but you need to determine if the client has approved the budget by asking is the required finance in place and are the executives willing to spend the budget to resolve this specific problem. The team needs to know what the client processes are that must be handled to get all the required signatures, and in addition, do you know all the approvals that are required?

Often the processes of the prospective client are in themselves a block to progress, so you need to decide what actions are in place to move the deal through the client's internal processes.

Documentation is critical, so are you sure the correct actions are in place to provide both you and the client with information, documentation, business case data, ROI, and so on?

By this stage, you will know who will be easy to negotiate with and who will be a nightmare. Decide now what actions to put in place to handle the most common negotiation tactics that you now will be using with the client.

5. The primary competition.

It is essential to know who the primary competition is and their real relationship with the client. Is the competition going after the same problems, and what tactics will they use, technically and commercially? Create a plan and actions that will create fear, uncertainty, and doubt for the competitor's solution, technology, and commercial viability.

You do not want a ping-pong match between the prospect, you, and the competition, so decide in advance of negotiations on the actions to put in place to avoid bake-off style comparisons. If that can't be avoided, then decide the actions and conversations to frame the discussion to your advantage. Correct pricing strategy is critical, so the team leader needs actions in place to handle the commercial strategies of the negotiation and be especially aware of the strategy the competition is likely to use.

Team Selling

Many people believe that selling is a team sport. While it feels like that is a true statement, all the psychometric evidence points to the top performers being team leaders, but not team players. There is a team of multifunctional expertise around them, but a successful salesperson knows that they must lead and drive that team. To do this, they must understand the basics of how teams operate. There is not enough time and space to cover this vast subject in this book. I recommend reading Natalie Dawson, *TeamWork: How to Build a High-Performance Team.*

However, it is worth identifying the difference between a team and a group. The salesperson can have a huge impact on creating a team effort but must be able to recognize when teamwork does not exist and what they must do about it to reach effective teamwork. This is a personal soft skill that all top sales performers possess. Figure 8.4 summarizes the key points.

The Working Group Key Elements

Look through this list and decide how many of these elements are currently in the team involved in your most recent live sale.

- Clearly focused leader
- Individual accountability

NOT ALL GROUPS ARE 'TEAMS' - HOW TO TELL THE DIFFERENCE...

"A team is a small number of people with complimentary skills who are committed to a common purpose, set of performance goals and approach for which they hold themselves mutually accountable" - Katzenbach and Smith - The Wisdom of Teams

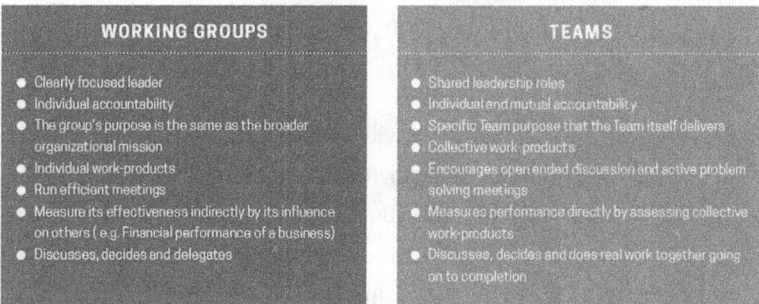

WORKING GROUPS	TEAMS
● Clearly focused leader	● Shared leadership roles
● Individual accountability	● Individual and mutual accountability
● The group's purpose is the same as the broader organizational mission	● Specific Team purpose that the Team itself delivers
● Individual work-products	● Collective work-products
● Run efficient meetings	● Encourages open ended discussion and active problem solving meetings
● Measure its effectiveness indirectly by its influence on others (e.g. Financial performance of a business)	● Measures performance directly by assessing collective work-products
● Discusses, decides and delegates	● Discusses, decides and does real work together going on to completion

Figure 8.4 Team selling. Not all groups are teams

- The group's purpose is the same as the broader organizational mission
- Individual work-products
- Run efficient meetings
- Measure its effectiveness indirectly by its influence on others (e.g., financial performance of a business)
- Discusses, decides, and delegates

This list looks ok, doesn't it? Well, it is not a team. It is a group of individuals, each with their own personal agenda. It reflects how most meetings operate in business today and why most attendees hate those meetings. What always happens in these groups is one person becomes the workhorse to get everything done or becomes the scapegoat for all the things that go wrong or tasks not completed. This is because tasks are delegated. There is accountability but only to the person to whom the task is given. The leader tends to dictate the tasks and delegate to the person least able to achieve the task or worse still the person who volunteers to do the task. There is no focus, and the group leader ensures they all follow the company themes. Problem solving, creativity, and innovation are lost. The blame game usually follows.

The definition of a team is they must have a common purpose and mutual accountability. The best definition of a team I have found is that a team is a small number of people with complementary skills who are committed to a common purpose, a set of performance goals, and an approach for which they hold themselves mutually accountable. This principle is clearly explained in the book by Katzenbach and Smith, *The Wisdom of Teams*.

Key Elements of Teams

Look through this list and you will immediately see the contrast to the elements in a group. Learn to identify these elements in a group of people brought together on your sale and be able to apply and create a team spirit to change them to an effective and productive team. Do research and create your own approach. It is critical to your sales excellence and success.

- Shared leadership roles
- Individual and mutual accountability
- Specific team purpose that the team itself delivers collective work-products
- Encourages open-ended discussion and active problem-solving meetings
- Measures performance directly by assessing collective work-products
- Discusses, decides, and does real work together going on to completion.

Proving and Progressing Tool Checklist

Ask yourself these critical questions. Have you:

- Established your solution is accepted by all stakeholders and buying committee?
- Ensured your business team has communicated the business value justification?
- Agreed the required client financial investment is approved and is available?
- Agreed and documented with your client the ROI?
- Agreed the compelling reason to act and identified client's predicted order date?
- Understood, aligned, and agreed the client decision process and sign-off process?
- Identified and confirmed with the client the steps and timings to purchase order?
- Quantified, shared and agreed the desired business outcomes of your solution?

If you can honestly answer "Yes" to all the previous questions then move on.

If you answer "No" to any one of the aforementioned questions then you must establish the reasons why and determine actions that will resolve the issues and progress the sale.

Linked to the previous checklist is the progress scorecard tool that I have redesigned and updated from my experience. It is used regularly by sales managers and sellers in my coaching sessions to review each forecasted sale. It has proved to be very effective. The tool has 10 key questions, and each question has five or six possible answers, which are quantified based on a probability factor of winning the sale. A total score is achieved, and if the total score is below 70 percent, then I know, after over 4,600 sales deal reviews, that the sale is highly likely to be lost unless the issues are fixed. The tool guides you through the process of how to identify actions that will fix the issue and progress the sale to a successful close. The original version of this tool began its life in my previous company, IBM, and I was given permission by my then VP to use and develop it in my ongoing independent coaching activities up to the present time. Over the years, I have amended, restructured, and changed the criteria and scoring system informed by research and my sales coaching experience to reflect today's sales dynamic environment. The progress scorecard tool is the result. The complete tool is download-able using a voucher from me from the link available in the Appendix. However, for brevity, in this chapter, I have concentrated on describing the 10 key questions that are critical to your success. In Chapter 11 there is a real example of applying the full progress scorecard tool.

Progress Scorecard Tool Questions

These questions are shown in Figure 8.5. You must be able to answer these questions positively. They are in order of importance based on buyer and sales research from multiple sources combined with my sales workshops feedback over the last eight years. These critical questions are often used independently as an important guide and reminder to any salesperson in their quest to progress their sale.

For example, when any seller I have coached cannot answer any one of the top three questions on the list then the sale is often lost or slips to the next quarter. Every seller must understand the desired financial business outcome and the compelling reason to buy.

It would be valuable for you to memorize these questions and apply them to every sale you have forecasted. Your answers will determine

Questions (in order of importance)
Who understands your projected Business Outcome, Return on Investment (ROI) & quantified client value?
What is the Compelling Reason that requires this opportunity MUST close when forecasted?
Have you asked the key stakeholders what can STOP our solution being implemented?
Who do you have a strong trusting relationship with?
Who have we agreed the buying process, milestones and timescales with?
What type of project Is our solution attached to?
What is the status of the clients Budget?
Are you in control of the Buying Criteria or Concept / Technology Proof?
What is the status of your solution versus the Competition?
Where are we with our Negotiation on pricing and terms?

Figure 8.5 Progress scorecard tool questions

the probability of selling successfully and inform your actions, and the questions will become an essential guide to consistent successful sales progression.

Case Study: Retail Giant

Transforming Company Performance

As in all the previous case studies, I am trying to highlight how the tool can act as a critical component. In this case, the progress scorecard tool clarified the major reason why the potential customer, who was leading retail store chain, had not yet agreed to go ahead with the deal. The seller, who was the key account manager of this important account, was convinced that he and his team had covered everything and did not know why he could not close the deal as forecasted. He agreed to complete the scorecard. To his surprise, he only scored 63 percent. I explained that any score under 70 percent means, in my experience, that the deal will not close when forecasted. He agreed that we analyze the answers. It quickly became clear what was missing. The questions are in order of importance. He was confident that all his decision makers and stakeholders understood and believed the projected business outcomes. However, he could not quote a compelling reason why they had to buy when he had forecasted. He admitted the customer had agreed to the timescales because the sales team needed the deal to close in this quarter. In addition, he had never asked the decision makers what could stop the deal from being implemented. Finally, he had not asked directly if the project was linked to an overall strategic business project. So, he went back and asked the questions.

It turns out that following the global COVID pandemic, the online business had tripled, causing the customers business model to be quickly changed. The company was re-engineering its whole retail strategy. The account manager knew this fact but realized he had not integrated his specific solution into the overall need to change company strategy nor had he shown how it would add value and be a critical component of that change. During his interview with each executive, his questions were guided by the progress tool, and he found those executives telling him exactly why they had stalled the deal. His team quickly rebuilt the proposal and pricing structure but critically highlighted how a new, earlier implementation timescale of their solution would rapidly help facilitate the completion of the overall company strategy. This is what the decision makers wanted to hear, and now reassured, they agreed to the deal two months earlier than forecasted.

CHAPTER 9

Negotiation and Agreement

How to Gain and Negotiate Agreement

In Chapter 2, we identified the eight 'hard' skills and why they need to be improved to gain sales excellence. In this chapter, we focus on negotiating the terms and conditions plus arranging the legal and implementation process that will reveal any weaknesses in your approach so far. If you have missed critical red flags and are not convinced by the decision makers of the value of your solution and your company, then those weaknesses will be exposed and exaggerated now. It is at this point in any sale that most sales are lost or slipped because what you missed previously will come back now to block your progress.

This chapter focuses on a unique methodology that you can learn, which applies sales excellence negotiation techniques and a powerful tool that will diagnose and remedy the remaining issues blocking your sale.

Negotiation and Agreement: Key Activities

The most important principle is to align your activities with that of your buyer and stakeholders. In your negotiating activities, you need to be aware that your potential customer has:

- Already developed their plan;
- Identified and analyzed the impact of any blockages that stop them from achieving their key strategic business objectives in their plan;

- Initiated a project to remove the blockages;
- Started to explore solutions from key vendors and suppliers;
- Evaluated your competitor's proposals and solutions;
- Proven the technology and the concept of the proposed solution;
- Now wants to agree to terms and conditions that are very favorable to their business.

Before you start agreeing to their demands and offering discounts, it would be best that you have checked that you have identified, qualified, and quantified the financial impact of the blockages on their business, discovered what the real value is to them for the blockages to be removed, demonstrated convincingly how and why your solution will transform their business, and started the proof of concept workshops with agreed criteria about the desired outcomes. Once these activities are completed and you are sure you are aligned with the buying process, only then can you start negotiating and agreeing to terms and conditions from a position of strength. The following techniques and tools will help you achieve that aim.

Buyer activities: Negotiate advantageous terms and conditions
Seller activities: Remove obstacles to the sale. Negotiate and agree on terms and conditions.
CRM stage: Customer acceptance.
SALES GOAL: Negotiate the completion of the sale. Share value documents and agree on client services and financial investment, process appropriate paperwork.

Negotiate to Win: Negotiation and Agreement

- Are you negotiating from a position of strength and confidence?
- Are you aligned with your buyer?
- Are you ready to defend your proposal and solution?

Negotiation and Agreement Activities Checklist

- Planned your negotiating strategy before final negotiations?
- Prepared and gained management approval for concessions?
- Agreed implementation and production timelines?
- Planned and agreed on "wants" from your potential customer?
  - What is mandatory to you?
  - What is our concession strategy?
  - Do you know the value for each concession?
  - Do you recognize the impact of making concessions too easily?
- Have you prepared to defend your proposition if the customer starts:
  - Demanding a further discount to the agreed figure.
  - Reducing the agreed value proposition terms and adding new requirements.
  - Reducing the value of the deal to all parties.
  - Bullying you for a better price and/or threatening to go to your manager.
  - Threatening to go to the competition.
- Have you created in advance ongoing calendar appointments to continue your negotiation defense strategy?

If you can honestly answer "Yes, I am doing this" to all the above activities, then you are ready to negotiate strongly and ask for the order. If you cannot answer "Yes" to all the above questions, then perhaps you might win the deal, but give away too many concessions, or find the deal slips into another quarter, or indeed lose the deal altogether. These techniques might help. They are followed by a key negotiation tool that will uniquely deliver value to both parties, combined with an environment of trust and calm, leading to a successful negotiation:

- **Call plan**
- **Objection skills**
- **Negotiation sheet**

Call Plan

The call plan in Figure 9.1 is one of three essential techniques that will prepare you for most negotiations. The questions in the call plan are designed to prepare you for a successful negotiation.

It is known and accepted by athletes and top sports people that it is critical to succeed in any sport, anticipating and preparing your mind for unexpected events is essential, and combining that with visualizing the exact movements or actions you plan to take will result in victory. Negotiation is no different. First, you must write down and prepare your terms in advance because the brain is geared to take notice of written-down data and views most of nonwritten data, for example, visual, as temporary until confirmed and reinforced by events. In addition, any negotiation always has unexpected twists and turns and demands. Trained negotiators know that if there is a want that they "give," it is on condition they receive an equivalent "get." Completing the sections in Figure 9.1 and inputting the expected will highlight and prepare you for the unexpected.

By preparing and writing down your positioning statement, you will know how to reinforce the value you bring to the sale. It also acts as your opening statement to begin the negotiation, if required. Knowing your walkaway terms is the next critical piece. If you are not able to walk away from this negotiation because, for example, you know that if you lose this deal you will be below the revenue target and possibly lose your job, then you are obviously not in a strong position to resist customer's demands for discounts and so on. Never go into a negotiation unless

Organization Name:			Opportunity:
Speaking To (and their role):			Date:
Key Decision Maker(s)			Agreement Needed By:
Decision Influencer(s)			
Optimal Outcome of this Call:			
Opening Offer Terms:		Walkaway Terms:	
Positioning Statement (Reinforce Business Value):			
Prioritized Customer Wants (Gives):	Underlying Customer Needs:	Gives we would offer:	Rationale (Gets):
Closing Statement I will Use to Recommend Moving to Next Stage of Sales Cycle:		My Plan if the Customer Replies in the Negative:	
Document Next Steps:			

Figure 9.1 Call plan

you are in a strong position to walk away, but if you are not able to walk away, then it is even more imperative that you plan and prepare. Finally, always know in advance your planned "next steps," and never leave until the next steps are agreed. Document these and send them immediately to the potential customer.

The above are the essentials to successful negotiation. However, if we are honest about it, most salespeople just try to wing it and hope for the best with the only goal being to get the order at any price. The techniques described are an attempt to make sure the basics are covered in all your negotiations.

Now we come to the most important and most common block to a good negotiation. How to handle pushback and demands from potential customers. We usually view them as objections to the sale. They are not objections at all, but a good sign that the potential customer wants to buy from you. They are, in fact, buying signals and a chance to progress the negotiation and win the sale. For example, if your partner is shouting at you and complaining, why do psychologists say this is a good thing? It is because that means they care. If your partner is very quiet and does not say anything, particularly when there has been an argument about something important, then it means they don't care or are too angry to talk or object. In sales, and in life, objections are the positive opportunities to make progress in any situation by applying the objection skills as shown in Figure 9.2. On a personal note, I taught this technique to my wife, who said it positively transformed her relationships with her relatives and friends.

Objection Skills

It is important you follow the process exactly. It is not easy. It looks easy, but in practice, it is very difficult. When I describe what you need to do, you will understand.

First, when the person opposite to you brings up an objection, for example, they say, *we have decided it is too expensive and we cannot afford the disruption*, you must pause for at least five seconds, keep very quiet, look thoughtful, and then repeat the exact words; *you have decided it is too expensive and you cannot afford the disruption?*; and then wait for

WHEN YOU RECEIVE AN OBJECTION, USE THESE 5 STEPS.
REPEAT STEPS 1-3 UNTIL OBJECTIONS ARE ALL EXHAUSTED

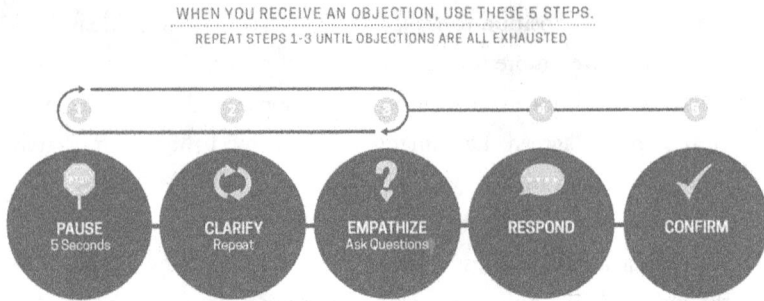

| PAUSE | CLARIFY | EMPATHIZE | RESPOND | CONFIRM |
| 5 Seconds | Repeat | Ask Questions | | |

Figure 9.2 Objection skills

an answer. It is common for a human being to respond to silence in a stressful situation by talking. Consequently, it is likely that you will get a response often before you have finished repeating their words. Once again, pause for at least five seconds, then repeat whatever they said back to them. Do this in your own personal way and don't appear robotic. Gradually, you will gain clarification about what they really want to object about and what they really want to achieve. At the point when they stop replying, you must then empathize with their situation. For example, *it must be disappointing that you will not be able to get the results you hoped to achieve.* You should always be empathic, thoughtful, and helpful. As shown in Figure 9.2, Steps 1 to 3 are repeated until you know it is time to respond positively with your proposal that you prepared in the call plan. It used to be called overcoming objections to get to a closing statement, but I think that is a poor reflection on what is happening. The focus here is on understanding and clarifying what the person is saying and being able to empathize and suggest a positive way of moving forward to help the person get the result they really want. It should always be a mutually beneficial process.

Negotiation Sheet

This technique depends on preplanning before the negotiation begins to achieve success. It also depends on you knowing why the potential customer is buying, what business problems they are trying to solve that you have discovered together during the sales process, and how you intend to achieve the desired objectives and business outcomes. That data need to be entered into the template (Figure 9.3).

In any sport, the winning team, in addition to good attacking strategy and skills, always practice and prepare defense techniques at length and as a priority. They know they will not win unless they defend when required. In negotiation, and as it happens in life situations, we call it making a stand. There are four key elements: plan, pain, value, and vision.

The examples shown in Figure 9.3 are taken from deals that were negotiated successfully. The strategy is to be prepared to resist buyer squeeze with this completed preplanned interactive negotiation worksheet and anticipate at least three demands with three defensive stands.

Here are examples from a real negotiation.

Stand 1: Plan Example

Our agreed plan shows an implementation date starting on May 10. Is this issue worth the delay?

Stand 2: Value Example

The reason we spent the last four months together is because you are not meeting your new account target. That Issue will not go away until you gain these new capabilities.

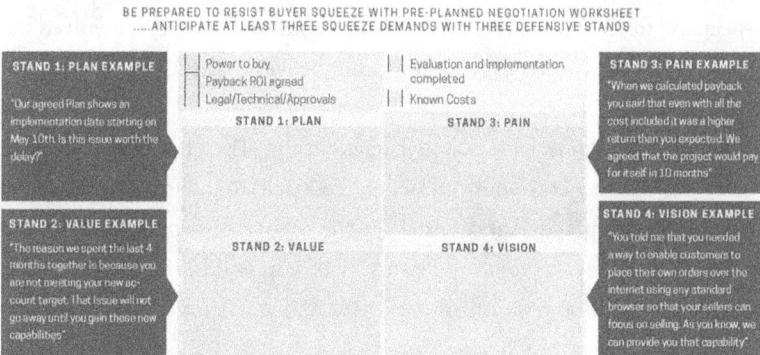

Figure 9.3 Negotiation sheet

Stand 3: Pain Example

When we calculated the payback, you said that even with all the costs included, it was a higher return than you expected. We agreed that the project would pay for itself in 10 months.

Stand 4: Vision Example

You told me that you needed a way to enable customers to place their own orders over the internet using any standard browser so that your sellers can focus on selling. As you know, we can provide you that capability.

Once you have completed your defensive strategy, then it is important to again be totally honest and ask yourself these questions:

- Does the person I am negotiating with have the power to buy?
- Have all stakeholders agreed with the payback figures in the return on investment business document we shared?
- Is evaluation and implementation plan completed and agreed?
- Are all the legal and technical approvals obtained?
- Do we know the definitive costs to us as well as the potential customer?

In the template, you must have all the boxes ticked before you step into the negotiation.

With all the above in place, you will be better prepared than your competition and be ready to accommodate and deal with any surprises, especially from senior executives, who tend to become reinvolved at this stage in the sales process and can be very disruptive if you are unprepared.

Finally, we come to the actual negotiation. The checklists and tool below have been created from seller feedback following hundreds of negotiations in practice and based on the theory of negotiation. If you are not able to say yes to all the items, then you will be walking into the negotiation from a position of weakness and not strength. That fact is the one key reason why negotiations fail.

Negotiation and Agreement Tool Checklist

Ask yourself these critical questions. Have you… :

- Agreed a negotiating and give-get strategy with your sales manager(s);
- Established a strong negotiating position to restate client business value confidently;
- Prepared the defense of your client value proposition and client value;
- Decided we can walk away and can reach quota without this sale;
- Confirmed your key contacts have power to sign purchase order, approve contract;
- Presented the final PO document and/or contract for signature;
- Completed the legal agreement, technical evaluation, implementation plan;

If you can honestly answer "Yes" to all the above questions, then move on.

If you answer "No" to any one of the above questions, then this tool will help.

Negotiation and Agreement Tool

This tool is based on the idea from a great book series called *The Go-Giver* by Bob Burg. I read this powerful story and business idea with great excitement and applied the principle to the negotiation stage of any sale. The tool is in the format of an interactive PDF using Adobe Pro. You can input live data and then feed it into your Customer Relationship Management (CRM) System.

It is critical when negotiating that when your potential customer asks for something more, for example, more discount, free support, and so on, and you are keen to close the deal quickly, don't be tempted to say yes immediately. "To give, you need to get" is the principle. There follow examples of how you can apply this technique very successfully so both parties feel that the negotiation has been mutually beneficial (Figure 9.4).

SELLER PRIORITY	GET			GIVE		PROJECTED CUSTOMER PRIORITY
	ELEMENT	POTENTIAL £€	POTENTIAL £€	ELEMENT		
1						1
2						2
3						3
4						4
5						5
6						6
	SELLER NON-NEGOTIABLES			CUSTOMER NON-NEGOTIABLES		

Figure 9.4 Give-get terms tool

Case Studies

Examples of using the give-get principle. This real example in Figure 9.5 highlights the actions of the seller involved as they prepared for the negotiation. The technique was successful, and the sale was gained, the software was installed, and the customer confirmed they were very happy and provided three very good referrals. Critically, the customer received what they wanted.

The potential customer wanted special payment terms, training discounts, short-term licenses, refunds on the proof of concept workshops costs, and reduced software costs. In other words, a large discount from the original quote. Each give had a value and a cost to the vendor. There are always non-negotiable factors, and they need to be decided, written down, and committed to before walking into any negotiation. In this example, no discount on maintenance and no free consulting were critical for the seller's successful implementation.

The negotiation technique is to ask for a get, cost it in the same terms, and make it a condition of the gives. It is also important to agree with your manager the red lines that you will not cross, which we call the non-negotiables.

Here is another example of the give-get principle in practice, during a recent negotiation I was involved while coaching the sales team. The customer wanted a large discount and would not budge. They were very happy with the products, services, and planned installation but just could not afford the overall costs. The deal was in danger of slipping. So we suggested to them that since they were the leader in the financial world, would they agree if our marketing people could

Our Priority	GET			GIVE		Projected Customer Priority
	Element	Potential Value	Potential Value		Element	
1	Larger Volume deal	$100k	$15k	Payment terms/special financing		2
2	Become a reference	$?k	$20k	Training discounts		1
3	Lower cost of sales by avoiding Pilot	$5k	$10k	Short-term licenses		4
4	Referrals for new business prospects	$?k	$10k	Refund on proof of concept already conducted		3
5	Pay software cost for Phase II at same time as Phase I	$2k	$1k	Reduce software costs		5

Partner / Vendor	NON-NEGOTIABLES	Customer
Maintenance Discounts		
Free Consulting		

Figure 9.5 Give-get template example

organize an interview with the editor of the *London Financial Times* after the software was installed? We were very confident of the software and product capability, and they were very impressed by our confidence, and it helped close the deal. We asked if they would agree to highlight during the interview the key point that their company was very happy with the software and products bought from us and would confirm it was a key factor in helping transform their performance and efficiency to retain their leadership in their market. That had to be worth the same dollar value as the discount they wanted. This was agreed and everyone was happy. We received over 100 hot sales leads following the publication of the article!!

CHAPTER 10

Confirmation
and Implementation

How to Gain Confirmation of Value
and New Business From Successful
Implementation

Sales is a never-ending circle and not a straight line. When we gain the purchase order, we are technically at the end of the sale, but we are also at the beginning. There is an old saying, you cannot have a beginning if you do not have an end. But it is what you do now that might or might not start a new beginning. Firstly, it might be worth just checking that you have covered all the bases.

The most important principle is to align your activities with that of your buyer and stakeholders. In your activities before the final signatures are gained, what you need to be aware of is that your potential customer has:

- Been through the lengthy process of developing their plan, identifying and analyzing the impact of any blockages to stop them from achieving their key strategic business objectives in their plan
- Initiated a project to remove the blockages and started to explore solutions from key vendors and suppliers
- Evaluated your competitor's proposals and solutions,
- Proven the technology and the concept of the proposed solution,
- Agreed to the terms and conditions with you that are very favorable to their business

Before you start thinking about moving on to the next sale after the signature stage and leaving the implementation to the technical and installation teams, it would be best to check that you have become a trusted advisor to the customer and will complete the sale with trust, respect, and integrity. Ask yourself, are you able to return to the customer after implementation has taken place, and will you be able to check that the customer has been using your solution successfully for at least six months? Once you are sure you have developed that trust and you were aligned and involved every step of the way with the buying process, then you can start confirming that the expected value has been received and plan to return to the customer to ask for referrals to help guide you to new business opportunities with similar problems to their own. The following techniques and tools will help you achieve that aim of completing the circle and gaining new business.

Buyer activities: Contract signed; implementation ongoing; measuring business outcomes.

Seller activities: Contract signed; implementation and business outcomes confirmed.

CRM stage: Customer implementation.

SALES GOAL: Contract and PO signed; implementation completed; customer business outcomes confirmed; business value received; validated and so gained referrals.

Confirmation Checklist

Ask yourself these critical questions. Have you:

- Ensured purchase order and/or contract are signed by all required stakeholders?
- Validated the business objectives, business outcomes will be achieved?
- Resolved outstanding implementation issues, identified actions?
- Confirmed the customer "post go live" success measurements are in place?

- Reviewed the required team resources implementation is progressing successfully?
- Agreed on follow-up appointment date within three months, and is it confirmed?
- Gained at least three new business referrals to grow your pipeline?

If you can honestly answer "Yes" to all the above questions, then move on to the follow-up implementation activities suggested in this chapter. If any answer is "No," then create actions to resolve the issues. Go back to negotiation or progression checklist and tools and check your answers and actions are genuinely completed. Alternatively, apply the following technique.

Confirm Value

As you have seen earlier, even after the negotiation has gone well and you have the agreement, you can still lose the sale. The technique highlighted in Figure 10.1 is a good method to ensure that all is well, and you will receive the purchase order. It is derived from and dependent upon the insight tool in the discovery in Chapter 6. The example below is from a real deal and should be self-explanatory.

You must begin by restating the objective and establishing the key reasons for the purchase. Reinforcing the message is one of the key

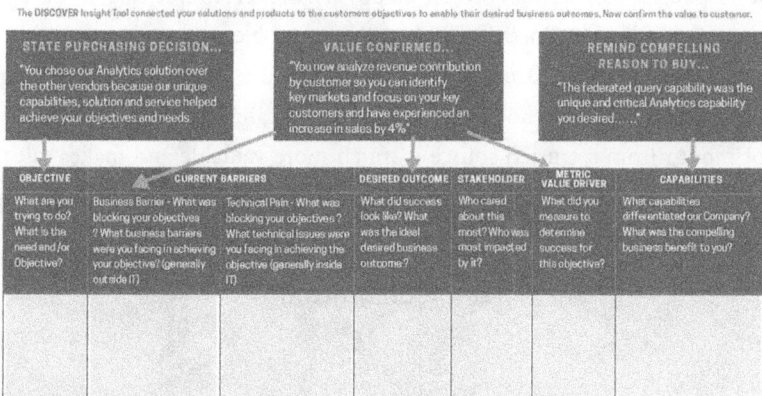

Figure 10.1 *Confirm value*

methods of obtaining excellence and success in any discipline, but especially in the skill of selling. Remind your potential customer of the business barriers that will be overcome. Detail again the desired outcomes stated and who cares about them most as stakeholders. Now highlight the method of measuring success that you have agreed with the customer after implementation. Finally, don't forget to state your unique differentiators in the market and your special capabilities to resolve their business problems with your product and services. State clearly the compelling financial benefits and outcomes to their company. These efforts will result in you not only getting the purchase order but also building trust and integrity, plus the very real chance of repeat business.

Once you are sure you are gaining the purchase order and it is confirmed, then supervising or at least keeping an overall involvement in the implementation of the product or solution into the customer's business model effectively is, I believe, still the responsibility of the salesperson. The top-performing salespeople always do this activity because it means they continue to win and build the trust of their customers. Many sellers leave the sale at this point and hand over completely to the admin, technical, and implementation team. This approach is often encouraged by sales management to quickly move on to win the next sale, but that is a big mistake. By keeping in touch with the customer's implementation status and helping to fix any issues, deep trust is established.

This means when the salesperson returns months later to see how it is going, they can ask their happy customer to provide three or more referrals of businesses they know have problems that their solution might be able to fix. Because there is continued trust, the customer will happily provide these hot leads. Research constantly confirms that word of mouth from a trusted source is much more valuable and makes sales more winnable than any leads from marketing campaigns.

Implementation

- Have you delivered value?
- Will you gain three valuable referrals?

Implementation Activities Checklist

- Are we confident that success will be achieved during the implementation process by following the agreed plan?
- Have you confirmed with the customer in writing that resources are aligned as contracted?
- Did you check with the key stakeholders that they continue to believe our solution provides value and desired business outcomes?
- Have you started the sales cycle again with stakeholders in other parts of the customers' organization and have we begun to develop business insights to related issues within the companies?
- Have you asked for recommendations and referrals?
- Have you agreed on a schedule of follow-up visits?

If you can honestly answer "Yes, I am doing this" to all the above activities, then you have, in effect, won trust with the purchase order and can move on with confidence to gain new business. If any answer is 'No', then you might ensure you gain and sustain future success by applying the following techniques.

Implementation Techniques

- **Implementation**
- **Referrals sheet**

The reason this activity is so important during the conclusion of the sale and afterward is that most of your competitor's sales teams will leave the sale immediately after the order is placed by the customer. This approach annoys customers because the team or person they have built up trust with has now gone. It is also wasting a genuine opportunity to be seen as providing excellence and great customer service from your company. More importantly, it misses a golden opportunity to gain new business by ensuring your customer is happy with their implementation. All it takes is continued contact and a minimum amount of the investment of your time. The reward of gaining new business is very high.

	Example			Complete below as per agreed proposal and purchase order		
ACTIVITY	DUE DATE	TEAM RESPONSIBILITY		ACTIVITY	DUE DATE	TEAM RESPONSIBILITY
Contract Agreement, Implementation Plan, Final legal and admin process begun	07/11	Tom , Seller, Bob Smith, legal Albert, Manager, Alfred, Sales Director				
Vendors, suppliers infrastructure plan, services ordered	23/11	Jim; Purchasing, Joshua Operations manager				
Services, Technical scoped and agreed	27/11	Andy Budget and John Smith Technical / Service teams				
Contract Signature – all legal done	03/12	Tom, Albert, Alfred, Bob Smith, Legal and Larry Benton – CEO authorised customer signatory				
Project kick-off Implementation	Proposing 19/12	Implementation Team				
Go live date	01/03	The Team				

Figure 10.2 Implementation

Implementation

Many sellers are actively encouraged by their managers to move on quickly once the sale is gained and the purchase order is confirmed. Most sellers agree that this is the correct strategy. This approach is a big mistake. The smart strategy is to remain involved in a small but tactical way to ensure what you sold is being implemented as planned. Visit the customer occasionally (Figure 10.2.)

Complete the template and share this document with the whole team. Once completed, then integrate the template within your CRM. You will be surprised how this is valued by others in the implementation team and shows you still care about your customer. Remember the time spent here will drive new business and new referrals in the future and will increase your credibility with your technical and support team. It is not wasted selling time, as some sales managers claim; it is an investment of your time to help you gain new business in the future.

Referrals Sheet

Finally, perform a quick checklist as suggested in Figure 10.3. It is a good memory jogger to do the things you keep putting off! The soft skill required at this stage is good time management. Create a time in your calendar every month to visit one customer that you recently sold to and has completed their implementation. The

SELLER ACTIONS	CHECK?
Has customer confirmed to seller that quantified desired Business Outcomes and the expected Value has been received?	☐
Have you established your company as the client standard supplier in your field of expertise?	☐
Written down contacts that must be visited in this account after the solution has been implemented and deployed?	☐
Decided how to leverage contacts built and how to extend the relationship?	☐
Designed message with purposeful questions to ask new customer who else in their organization would benefit from our solutions?	☐
New leads gained and have built additional quality Pipeline?	☐
Calendar appointment completed with each of the 3 new referrals.	☐
Confirm Client Value received with Post Call Tool completion?	☐

Figure 10.3 Referrals sheet

idea of this technique is that when you return to your customer after implementation, you are reminded of why you are spending time here and what your objectives are, making the visit valuable to both you and the customer.

If the above techniques and activities have not been possible due to time restraints or the fact you are always busy chasing other deals, then the tool shown in Figure 10.4 describes the minimum activity required after any sale. It is essential to carry out this activity for you to gain and sustain excellence and continue your sales success.

Postsales Checklist Tool

Go back to your customer and confirm everything in the template in Figure 10.4. Your goal is to build trust and gain three good referrals from a satisfied customer. Very few sales organizations, sales managers, account managers, or sellers carry out this task, claiming they do not have the time. By doing this activity regularly, you will differentiate yourself from the crowd, gain more new business, and sustain sales excellence.

CUSTOMER DETAILS AND ACTIVITY	CHECK?	SELLER CHECKLIST AND ACTIVITY	CHECK?
Organization Name and date sold in CRM?	☐	Follow up review date agreed?	☐
F2F with Key Decision Maker(s) in Sale?	☐	Objective of meeting established?	☐
F2F with Decision Influencer(s) in Sale?	☐		
Has customer confirmed and quantified expected Value has been received?	☐	Fully prepared to ask high yield questions to confirm value was received?	☐
Prepared top three questions and top three expected actions from customer?	☐	Prepared top three answers and top three expected actions required for customer visit?	☐
Questions Expected from Customer	☐	My Answers	☐
1.	☐	1.	☐
2.	☐	2.	☐
3.	☐	3.	☐
Expected Actions Required from Customer	☐	Planned Actions	☐
1.	☐	1.	☐
2.	☐	2.	☐
3.	☐	3.	☐
Three new leads or Referrals given?	☐	Closing Statement prepared that I will use to gain three Referrals?	☐
		Planned response if the Customer Replies Negatively?	☐
Confirmed business outcome and next steps?	☐	Next Steps documented?	☐

Figure 10.4 Postsales checklist tool

Case Study: How Returning to Check Value Received and to Confirm Successful Implementation Always Produced New Business

I feel this example is a good way to demonstrate why sales is a never-ending circle and not a straight line. We are technically at the end of the sale, but we are also at the beginning. This example is of a company in the Nordics. The sales team had never followed up on their sales because they had such a good implementation and technical team, whom they trusted, and did not feel the need to go back. However, I had been called in because their pipeline was gradually decreasing, and they needed new prospects. To their surprise, I asked them all to go back to their customers they have sold to over the last few years and apply the techniques in this chapter, especially the techniques in Figure 10.3 and Figure 10.4. They completed this action in record time. The reason was every time they visited an existing customer and applied the techniques in this chapter to confirm what they had purchased had produced the promised business outcomes, then they obtained at least three new business opportunities. The Nordic team doubled their pipeline and increased its quality significantly.

Many sales managers and salespeople think it is a waste of good selling time to back to their customers on the assumption that if they have not heard about problems and issues, then all is OK. Alternatively, the reason might be they are anticipating problems and want to leave it to technical to fix. It is often the case that customers will try to fix most of the issues on their own without complaining or will complain and get technical support to fix the issues. However, they will not be happy, and not only will they not buy again but they will quietly tell many of their colleagues in their industry and you will not know about that fact. Not all customers use social media to highlight shortcomings because it can reflect badly on their image and branding.

What transpired every time in the Nordics team was that the salespeople often discovered that there were multiple issues that had not been fixed or were ongoing. What impressed their customers was that rather than visiting just to look for new business, these sellers appeared to be genuinely interested in answering the question: Did it fulfill your expectations? The salespeople had a good relationship with their technical colleagues and directly ensured that any issues were resolved. It may look and sound simple, but this approach works. I am not recommending that sellers try to fix issues themselves, but I am recommending going back to your customers every time and supervising the resolution of those issues and then asking for three referrals to get possible new business opportunities. Just ask, do you know of anyone else experiencing the business problems we have solved? It is a good approach, and it works.

CHAPTER 11

Combining All the Ingredients

How to Sustain Sales Excellence

This chapter focuses on how to apply and execute successfully the sales excellence framework. Combining the 'hard' sales skills covered in the previous chapters with the human "soft" skills creates a self-coaching, interactive, practical self-coaching sales framework and methodology containing proven practitioner techniques and tools that will align you with your prospective customer at every stage of the buyer's purchasing process. This approach delivers results that go way beyond merely following your Customer Relationship Management (CRM) system and Artificial Intelligence (AI) data.

First, you must combine these "hard" sales skills with the critical "soft" human skills and embed them into your sales automation processes and methodologies. This will provide the crucial skills required and integrate them into a framework and methodology that creates predictable, repeatable sales results in our unpredictable world, consistently delivering the desired business outcomes for your customer.

Acquiring the "soft" skills to achieve business success in today's knowledge digital society is now equally as important as knowing how to apply the "hard" sales skills that enable you to know your customer needs and deliver the business and desired outcomes. I have taken my inspiration from *Teaching in a Digital Age* by Anthony William Bates.

Knowing what these skills are and how to integrate these essential soft skills into your sales processes and methodologies is paramount. First, we must identify and describe them.

Identifying the Human "Soft" Sales Skills: The Eight Soft Skills

1. Communication skills
2. Ability to learn independently
3. Applying ethical beliefs
4. Creating teamwork, collaboration, and flexibility.
5. Time management
6. Thinking skills
7. Digital and AI skills
8. Knowledge management

Communications skills: In addition to the traditional communication skills of reading, speaking, and writing coherently and clearly, we need to add social media communication skills. These might include the ability to create a short YouTube video to capture the demonstration of a process or to make a sales pitch, the ability to reach out through the internet to a wide community of people with one's ideas, to receive and incorporate feedback, to share information appropriately, and to identify trends and ideas from elsewhere.

Ability to learn independently: This means taking responsibility for working out what you need to know and where to find that knowledge. This is an ongoing process in knowledge-based work because the knowledgebase is constantly changing. Incidentally, I am not talking here necessarily of academic knowledge, although that too is changing; it could be learning about new equipment, new ways of doing things, or learning who are the people you need to know to get the job done.

Ethics and responsibility: This is required to build trust, particularly important in selling and operating in social networks, but also because generally it is good business in a world where there are many different players and an increased degree of reliance on others to accomplish one's own goals. Salespeople are often accused of being immoral, untrustworthy, and lacking in a basic sense of responsibility. I would say from my experience and from most of the sales research that the most successful salesperson is the one most trusted and, like all good friends, is the one who challenges the customer because they care as much about the business outcome of their solution, product, or service as do their customers. Top performers have a deep sense of morality and responsibility. They are always the longest-serving, the most reliable, and the most consistently successful of any sales force. Untrustworthy and unreliable salespeople may be on target or above for a short time, but their average tenure in a company is around 12 to 18 months. Sales managers and executives need to be wary of this type because in today's digital world, the research contained in the book *Virtual Selling* by Shultz, Shaby, and Springer shows that only the trusted advisor consultative seller will survive and be successful in the sales teams of today and of the future.

Teamwork and Flexibility: Although many knowledge workers work independently or in very small companies, they depend heavily on collaboration and the sharing of knowledge with others in related but independent organizations. In small companies, it is essential that all employees work closely together, share the same vision for a company, and help each other out. Knowledge workers need to know how to work collaboratively, virtually, and at a distance with colleagues, clients, and partners. The pooling of collective knowledge, problem-solving, and implementation requires good teamwork and flexibility in taking on tasks or solving problems that may be outside a narrow job definition but necessary for success. In the sales profession, this ability is critical. Salespeople tend not to be team players. However, the successful salesperson of today has learned to curb their independent streak and become part of the team, but as the leader of the team. A successful salesperson is never a follower.

Thinking skills: Of all the skills needed in a knowledge-based society, these are some of the most important. Businesses increasingly depend on the creation of new products, services, and processes to keep down costs and increase competitiveness.

Universities have always prided themselves on teaching such intellectual skills, but the move to larger classes and more information transmission, especially at the undergraduate level, challenges this assumption. Also, it is not just in the higher management positions that these skills are required. Tradespeople and business professionals are increasingly having to be problem-solvers rather than following standard processes, which are quickly becoming automated with AI now leading the way. Anyone dealing with the public needs to be able to identify needs and find appropriate solutions. Sales professionals have traditionally not been recruited for their thinking skills but have been recruited for their get-up-and-go and never-give-up mentality. They believe *no* means *perhaps* and is merely a sign that they should sell, sell, sell until the customer agrees and buys. This is changing. The soft skills of critical thinking, problem-solving, creativity, originality, and strategizing are now critical to sales success.

Digital and AI skills: Most knowledge-based activities depend heavily on the use of technology. However, the key issue is that these skills need to be embedded within the knowledge domain in which the activity takes place. This means, for instance, real estate agents knowing how to use geographical information systems to identify sales trends and prices in different geographical locations; welders knowing how to use computers to control robots examining and repairing pipes; and radiologists knowing how to use new technologies that read and analyze MRI scans. Salespeople need to know much more than what to do and why they are doing it but need to know how to apply knowledge gained from new automated sales support systems and combine them practically with their knowledge of the psychology of influence, decision making, and human engagement. Thus, the use of digital technology needs to be integrated with and evaluated through the knowledgebase of the subject area. This especially applies to AI skills. In a recent interview on BBC Radio 4 Brian Cox, a world-famous scientist, was quoted as saying, AI does not know or use or understand human emotion in decision making. AI supports decision making but cannot make decisions. That is still the role of human beings and is still the role of professional salespeople of supporting the making of decisions in the selling/buying decision-making process.

- An example of how a knowledge worker like a salesperson can apply technology as a support tool is AI. Often in the sales process, sellers find themselves stuck because they are lacking data on their prospective customer. For example, they know they need to do more research but cannot find the time and do not really know how to read and interpret a corporation's annual financial report. When this happens, the salesperson needs help. They will increasingly turn to a search engine with AI. But the key benefits of AI only come when you ask the right question to get the correct and accurate answer. Many CRM systems claim they can help and are trying to add AI tools. However, each sales situation is unique since the seller is trying to influence and guide the buyer to decide in their favor. Often the CRM data are not accurate and deliver the wrong answer due to being asked the wrong question. The sales excellence framework guides you to the relevant sales skills section and highlights the key questions you need to ask to do successful research on the potential customer. The framework uses the checklists that guide you to ask the right questions on your AI tool. So let's say you are using Gemini AI, and the framework guides you to ask, Gemini, give me a concise summary of the profit and loss account of XYZ corporation. If it is a public company, then you will receive an instant report that is accurate and gives you the financial data you need. If it is a private company, then you will receive a comprehensive but not accurate or validated report. It will be useful, but you must do further research. You can then integrate that data into your CRM and deal framework to inform your discussions with your prospective customer.

This will differentiate you as a valuable resource and sales professional.

Knowledge management: This is perhaps the most overarching of all the skills. Knowledge is not only rapidly changing with new research, new developments, and rapid dissemination of ideas and practices over the internet, but the sources of information are increasing, with a great deal of variability in the reliability or validity of the information. Thus, the knowledge that an engineer learns at university can quickly become obsolete. There is so much information now in the health area that it is impossible for a medical student to master all drug treatments, medical procedures, and emerging science such as genetic engineering, even within an eight-year program. The key skill in a knowledge-based society is knowledge management: how to find, evaluate, analyze, apply, and disseminate information, within a specific context.

This is a skill that many professional sellers require as a must-have because they need to access and assimilate huge quantities of knowledge. Indeed, many business and MBA graduates from top universities are learning that to be successful in their business careers and in life, they will need to employ and improve this skill that top salespeople have perfected. In his book *To Sell is Human*, Daniel H. Pink highlights and states that we are all in sales now. He writes that according to the U.S. Bureau of Labor Statistics, one in nine Americans works in sales. Every day more than 15 million people earn their keep by persuading someone else to make a purchase. But he says dig deeper, and a startling truth emerges: Yes, one in nine Americans works in sales. But so do the other eight. Whether we're employees pitching colleagues on a new idea, entrepreneurs enticing funders to invest, or parents and teachers cajoling children to study, we spend our days trying to move others. Like it or not, we're all in sales now. This is developing into a global phenomenon as new digital technologies and knowledge advance rapidly throughout the business world.

Each tool and technique used to improve and gain the eight "hard" sales skills in the previous chapters has been integrated with the above eight "soft skills" to create an interactive self-coaching framework, shown and highlighted in Figure 11.1, that sustains your sales excellence and drives you to become a consistent top performer in your sales team. The framework is applied to each ongoing top sales deal you are working on and provides key data that are accurate and relevant that you input into your CRM and AI tools.

Combining the Ingredients to Sustain Sales Excellence

Applying the sales excellence self-coaching framework

> Step 1. Diagnose the deal. Apply the sales excellence framework checklists.
>
> Step 2. Decide which technique and tool to use. Apply the specific technique and tool to gain and sustain sales excellence.

Imagine the usual sales situation. A hot lead has come from marketing, or you have been approached by an existing customer, or your inbound sales team has revealed a good prospect, or you have received a request for pricing. Whatever the source you have likely already contacted the prospect, asked lots of questions using your CRM and AI tools, described your solution, demonstrated it over Zoom or, if you are lucky, face-to-face, then sent a proposal as requested by the customer. You have confidently forecasted the sale and added it to your CRM. However, the sale is now not going so well. Complications have developed. Your decision makers and your key contacts turn out to not have the authority to sign or produce the purchase order, nor are your key contacts as influential as you had been led to believe. Your sale is slipping away from you, and you might even lose it. Your manager is now involved, but he cannot stop the prospective customer from delaying or postponing key planned meetings. This is usually where things become even more complicated. The sale is lost to competition, or slipped from the forecasted quarter, or lost completely with the prospect deciding to do nothing. As a result, the sales revenues are not as forecast. The sales team is underperforming, and win rates are falling. I am often called in to companies to help or advise in these situations. I am asked to advise the company salespeople, managers, or sales coaches. We start by applying the framework in Figure 11.1 to lost, slipped, or

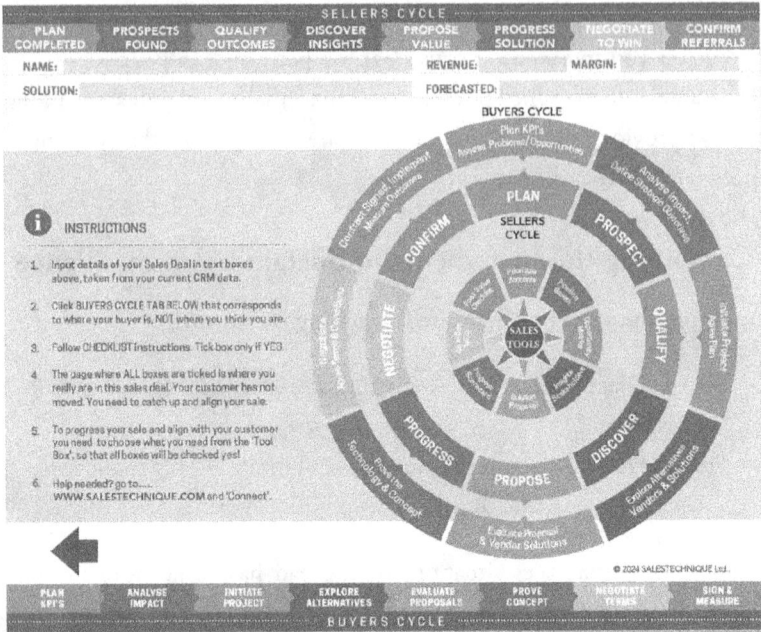

Figure 11.1 The sales excellence framework

ongoing deals. Then we apply the method to find new business and create accurate forecasts.

First, we need to check that you are aligned with the stakeholders and buyers, and you are where you think you are in the sales process and your sales forecasts. Next, we identify the blockages that are preventing the sale from progressing. Finally, we need to be able to take remedial action quickly and effectively by applying the tools and techniques and then recording the outcomes in your CRM to produce accurate CRM data.

For example, you are selling to a nationwide construction company and have forecasted a $100k sale to be signed in April. It is now February. This deal has already slipped from the last quarter in the previous year because the main contact in your prospect communicated to you at the beginning of December that the CEO had blocked all future purchases till the following year so that he could maximize profit in the annual report to his shareholders and investors. This action surprised and frustrated you and embarrassed your manager, who had forecast the deal to his manager. In addition to this construction company deal, you have two further deals that have slipped from last year into this year, these being an oil company and an Electricity Generating Renewables Company, both nationwide enterprises. These are the top of your target list in your territory and vertical market, and you will not achieve your sales target unless you sell to them.

The strategy and process we use to help you achieve these sales and reach sales excellence are as follows. You download a new framework for each opportunity and complete the front page sections as in Figure 11.1, taking the data from your CRM for each opportunity. You now have three separate self-coaching frameworks on each deal that will provide a unique bespoke set of solutions and actions that will guide you through the sales process, provide accurate data for your CRM, and enable you to accurately forecast and win all three deals.

Sustaining Sales Excellence: Applying the Sales Excellence Self-Coaching Framework

The framework has two distinct interconnected functional parts that must be carried out in sequence. The first step is applying the checklists that diagnose and identify, like a doctor, the blocks to your deal affecting the health of the process. The next step is to remove those blockages to your sale and be realigned with your stakeholders and buyers. Lastly, the data and actions are then entered into your CRM to establish the accuracy of forecasting. The questions contained in the checklist, tools, and techniques are used to inform your AI tools. As we discussed in Chapter 1 and earlier when we highlighted the crucial soft skills you need to develop in today's digital world, you must ask the right question to get the right answer when using AI tools.

Example 1

Let's First Focus on the Construction Company Example.   The stage when the sale slipped was negotiation. In Chapter 9, we developed and discussed in detail how to improve the "hard" skill of negotiation. It is time now to apply what we have learned, and first, you must establish if you are ready to negotiate. The customer is ready, but are you? The research we discussed in Chapter 1 revealed that one of the key factors that cause sellers to lose their sale is they were never aligned with their stakeholders and buyers. The consequence of this could be the sale was never qualified at the beginning of the sale, and you never really discovered the financial impact of the company's declared problems. The seller may have been so intent on winning that they missed the facts that, for example, their customer was not happy, the risk was too high for them, or they were just not ready to buy. Is this the case with the construction company? Let's find out. The deal stalled at the negotiation stage, so you click on the negotiate to win box shown in Figure 11.1. This brings up the negotiation stage checklist with questions we learned how to use in Chapter 9. Honesty with yourself is critical. In this example of the construction company, Figure 11.2 shows clearly which boxes the seller could honestly tick and which ones they could not.

Any unticked box means the seller was not ready to negotiate. The customer is ready, but you are not aligned. What did you miss? You

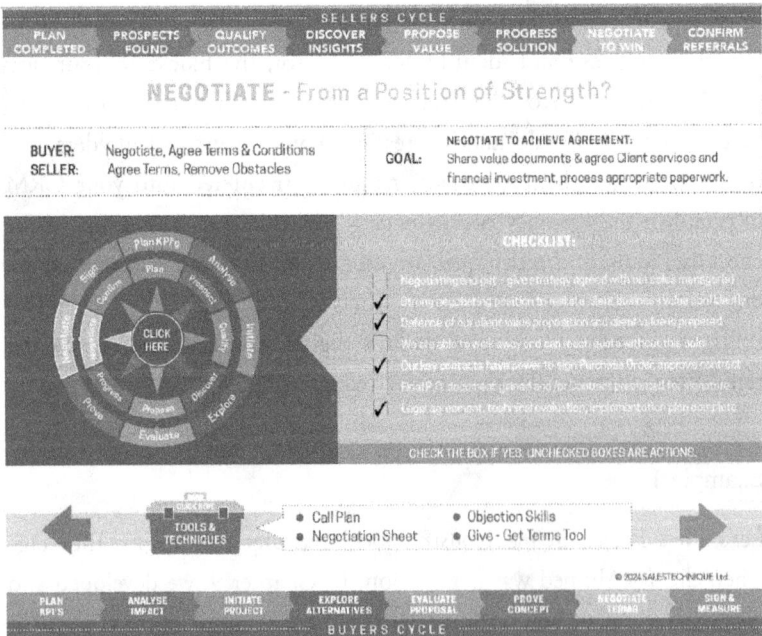

Figure 11.2 The negotiation checklist: Example 1

must go back, but you cannot time travel. However, you could fix the issues if you knew specifically what they are. The framework provides a method. Go back by clicking on the arrow indicating back. We are now in progress solution examined in detail in Chapter 8. The seller once again ticked the boxes but could not tick all of them for this stage. The seller could not tick the box that asked, is there a compelling reason to act and is a predicted order date agreed? It is important to go back again. We now arrive at proposed value. Once again the seller could not tick all the boxes and left two unticked. They did not quantify the alternative of doing nothing and did not articulate that question to the prospect. In addition, the key decision makers had not agreed the proposal achieved their desired business outcomes. The sponsor and influencers had agreed, and so too did many of the users, but not the key decision makers. Once again we go back. We are now at one of the most important stages and skill sets of any sale. How do you discover the full extent of the business problem and its impact? The checklist exercise revealed that this time we had three missing key

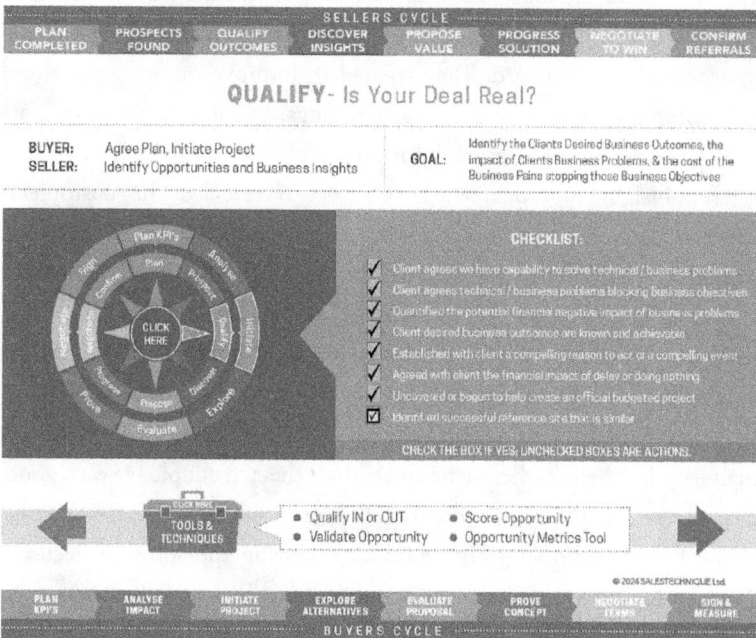

Figure 11.3 The qualification: Example 1

factors highlighted by unticked boxes. The seller had not captured the desired strategic business objectives, nor established how the customer was going to measure the performance, nor how the success of the solution being presented after installation was going to be measured. More importantly, the compelling event or compelling reason to act had not been established. The seller must go back. The next stage is qualification, detailed in Chapter 5. Now, all the boxes were confidently ticked by the seller, as shown in Figure 11.3.

This means that the seller is at the stage of discovery, but the customer is still at the stage of negotiation. The seller is therefore not aligned with the buyer, and that is probably why the sale has stalled. As detailed in Chapter 6, we now need to identify the blocks, then resolve and remove them. So, we now click on the forward arrow to reveal what to do about discovering why the customer wants to buy and what do they value as a desired business outcome. The framework guided the seller to use the discovery insights tool. It was recorded in the CRM that the project director of the company, who was a key contact and stakeholder, had communicated that the job costing software licenses they were using ran out of contractual support for their 65 job costing analyst users at the end of the year, and so the contract had to be renegotiated and renewed. They wanted to improve the software; there were some increasingly serious shortcomings, but it was doing the job quite well and was good enough for now.

The insight tool detailed in Chapter 6 revealed the customers' answers, who, with the seller and me, had now completed the tool face-to-face. In their own words, the tool revealed what they were trying to do as a key business goal at that specific time of the year was reduce costs and maximize profit. The tool revealed that their technology was, in fact, stopping them from achieving their secondary key goal of increasing the abilities and accuracy of their 65 financial planning analysts. So their earlier statement that their technology was good enough was, in fact, not true. The Insights tool highlighted the costs of the failing technology. In addition, renewing the software licenses, a reason for buying that the seller believed was compelling, was not, in fact, a compelling reason to buy. It was clear that if the customer did not renew the licenses, they felt they would manage any outages, and so doing nothing would not cost them much, but buying the software impacted and reduced the company's net profit that the CEO had forecast. The CEO did not know their technology was lacking in key abilities and was, in fact, costing them significant money, as revealed by the framework tools. Had the seller discovered these issues and costs earlier and linked the new technology they were selling to the business outcome goal of increased profit, then perhaps a solution could have been found that satisfied the CEO, and the deal could have been closed in the forecasted month.

Interestingly, over the next few months, the framework tools became so popular with the customer that it provided the ability and actions for the seller and the support team to address the other issues revealed by the framework that they had been unaware of and so resolved many issues in advance. As a result, the sale was now forecasted for March, and indeed, the sale was gained in March. Check out Chapter 6 to remind yourself how the insights tool could help you.

This example may appear simple, and you may feel the seller should have been able to anticipate the issue, but the potential customer often says their technology is good enough and renewals of software often stall. The result is the deal gets delayed from quarter to quarter, but as you can see, this is easily avoidable. Had the seller been aware of the CEO's goals and applied the sales excellence framework techniques and tools in their research at the planning, prospecting, and qualification stages, then they would have been able to anticipate and resolve issues before they became blockages. Their forecast would have been accurate, reliable, and predictable. That is the hallmark of a top performer who has attained and can sustain sales excellence.

The oil company and another company in electricity generating renewables had issues that were very different.

Example 2

The Oil Company Was a Major National Company That Operated Globally. Like many in their industry, they were divesting old technology and acquiring companies with new technology. Their strategic business objective was to integrate these disparate operations into one financial model to be able to manage and control profitable growth. However, the seller, who was the key account manager of this enterprise, only discovered this significant fact after the deal had slipped out of their forecast. I had been called in to coach the sales team. I started a one-to-one session with the account manager of the oil company.

The account manager had been approached by the head of financial planning of the oil company to quote for a new financial planning system. The deal could be worth hundreds of thousands of dollars. Even though the seller was very experienced, he became very excited by the opportunity, not least because he was behind in his annual sales target. He quickly sent a full quote and then arranged a demonstration for the sponsor and stakeholders, but not the decision makers. The seller assumed that he was trusted by his sponsor, the head of financial planning, who had the trust of the divisional decision makers.

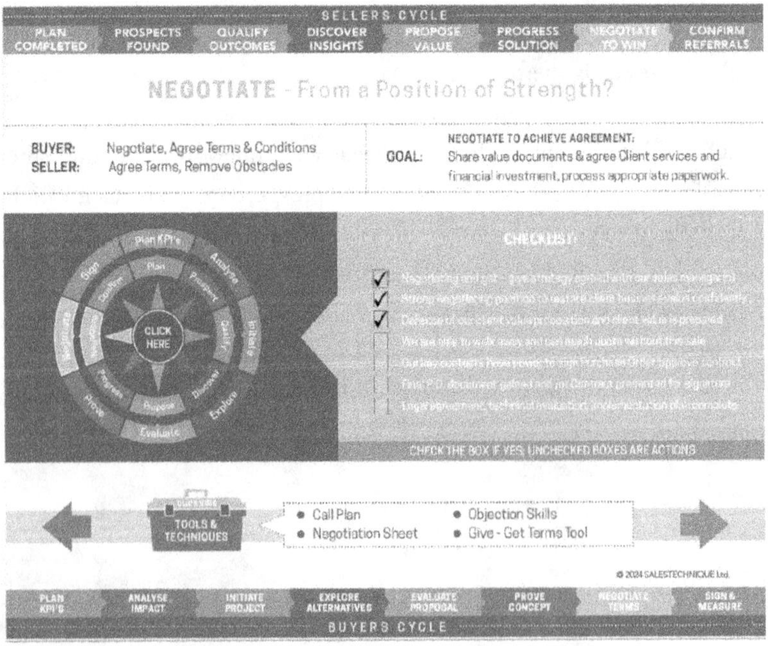

Figure 11.4 The negotiation: Example 2

We applied the framework using at first the account manager's CRM notes. Once again, the seller had been at negotiation stage when the deal had slipped. So that's where we started. Figure 11.4 highlights the answers.

As you can see, the seller was nowhere near being able to negotiate from a position of strength. He was behind target, so he could not walk away from the deal. He was therefore too ready to discount, which was a red flag to the customer. He did not have direct contact with the decision makers who signed the purchase order. As a result of his overconfidence, no final contract or document had been prepared, nor had the legal, technical, and implementation details planned. The framework guided the seller back to each stage, and at each stage, the seller had items missing that were critical. We eventually arrived at qualification. Remember the prospective customers and buyers are still at their negotiation stage, having decided what they want to buy. The seller now needs to catch up and work to highlight to his key account contacts what, why, and how he can help them achieve their desired

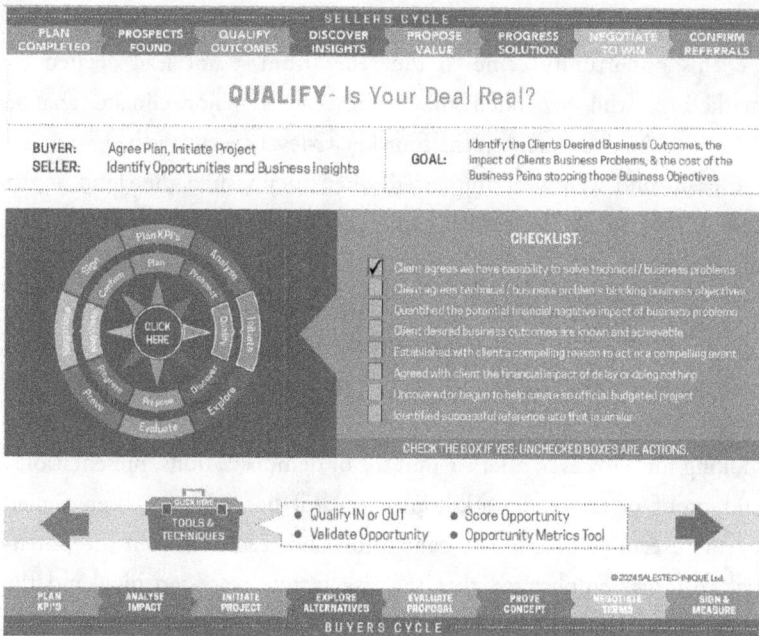

Figure 11.5 The qualification: Example 2

business outcome of collating their financial planning into one system to allow accurate budgeting.

Figure 11.5 shows clearly what was missing way back at the beginning of the sale. The account manager had not qualified the deal at all and should never have responded to the customer's request for a quote and demonstration, even though he felt trusted and knew his account well. There is a golden rule in selling. Discovery before demonstration. Overconfidence is a common fault with experienced key account managers. As you can see, only one box is ticked, and so the account manager had made many assumptions, which caused him to slip up much later in the deal and was the key reason for the deal slipping. In fact, he eventually lost the deal to competition.

Example 3

The Electricity Generating Renewables Company Reasons for not Buying and Delaying the Purchase Were Very Different From the Previous Two Examples. This example highlights how valuable the framework's techniques and tools can become in helping to deliver accurate forecasting and winning your sale.

This opportunity came to the seller from a hot lead created by marketing, who generated the interest at a major climate change exhibition and conference. The four key C-level executives had attended the event and were very impressed when they visited the stand at the exhibition and by the speech given at the opening of the conference by the marketing director of the seller's company, who are leaders in their technological field. The chief exective officer (CEO), chief operating officer (COO), chief technology officer (CTO), and chief revenue officer (CRO) all had reasons to progress their interest because the technology being offered seemed to be exactly what they were looking for. However, after six months of demonstrations, presentations, and proof of concept workshops, the deal had still not been signed by the executive board. The conclusion and feedback from the potential customer emphasized that the risk factors were too high and the purchase and running costs could not be justified at the time for this fast-growing renewable company. There were also other more important company priorities that came first. They had decided to stick with the technology they were using. It was good enough. A comment we have heard before and often hear in sales. I was called in to help.

Once again, because this is another deal that was forecasted and slipped. The stage we are at is negotiation. As you can see from Figure 11.6, when we completed the checklist using the data from the CRM, the sales team was, in fact, not ready to negotiate and had to go back and discover what sales factors were missing.

In this example, the sales team was very confident, and the seller was particularly happy because they were in direct contact with the decision makers and there was an evident good relationship that had developed. So, what was going wrong? The sales team and seller did not agree with the result of the negotiation checklist. They did not feel they needed to have a give-get strategy, nor restate the client value, nor defend their value proposition. Although the final documents had not been presented, it was felt that it was only a matter of time and

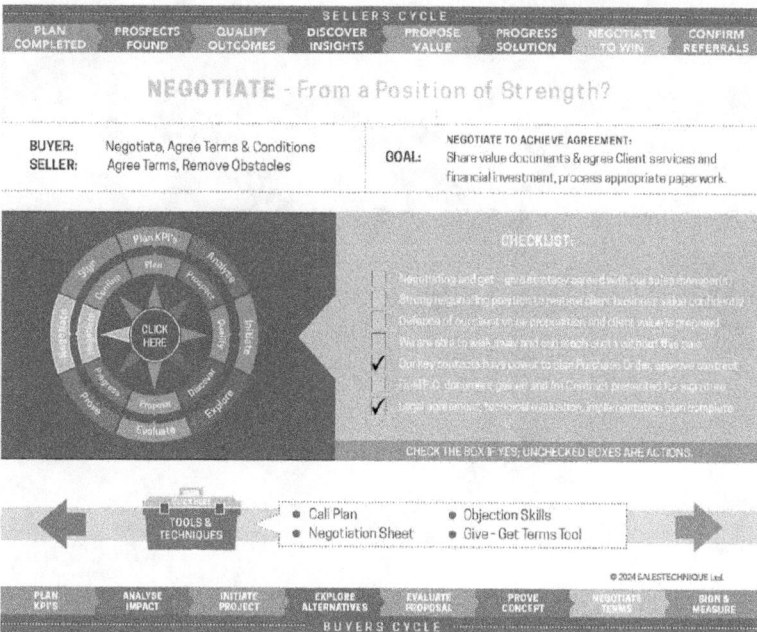

Figure 11.6 The negotiation: Example 3

would be happening soon. However, as it turned out, that was not the potential customers' view of things.

The seller and the team agreed reluctantly to complete the framework checklist. So, taking the data once again from the CRM, we hit the back arrow. It is worth looking at what was missing. Figure 11.7 clearly shows the problems. The team is still not aligned with the buyer's or customer's needs.

In contrast to what the seller and sales team thought they had achieved, they admitted that the business outcomes of their solution after implementation had not been quantified, shared, or agreed upon in the potential customer's own financial term. This task is the last checklist question but one of the most important to progress any sale successfully. The team also realized that they could not say definitively that all stakeholders and buying committee had accepted the solution. Finally, the return on investment had never been accepted in writing, and there was no compelling reason to buy on the date that the team had forecasted the sale. The seller and the team agreed to hit the

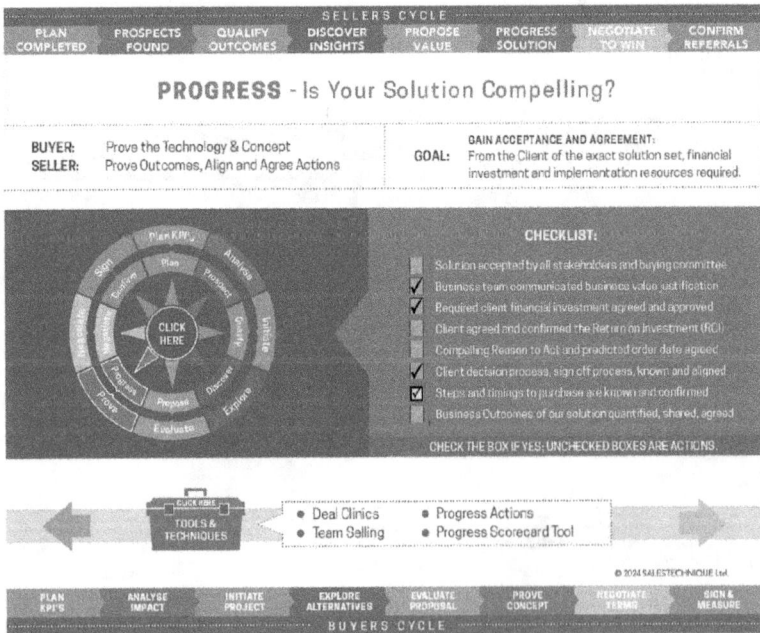

Figure 11.7 The progression: Example 3

back button in the framework and then ticked all the checklist boxes, convincing themselves that they had the correct proposal, knew the value the customer wanted from their technology, and were sure the opportunity was well qualified.

As a sales coach and previously as a company executive and sales leader, I have heard these confident comments and excuses many times from experienced sellers and sales teams. It causes major issues at sales review sessions, and often senior managers become involved to try to push the deal forward. The ends-justify-the-means approach is used because it is a major forecasted deal. Expectations are raised, promises are made, discounts are offered, and other concessions are tried and pushed hard, which sometimes work, but in the main, this approach causes pushback and suspicion from the potential customer. If problems occur later in the implementation, then an unhappy and suspicious customer is not easy to gain co-operation. The sale can easily become a nonprofitable situation.

Experience and hundreds of coaching sessions and workshops have proven that the framework, techniques, and tools, when applied correctly, will consistently help sales teams and sellers avoid these pitfalls. At the beginning of this chapter, we discussed the eight "soft" skills. They are all contained in the framework techniques and tools. I want to highlight how these soft skills are integrated and embedded in the framework using these latest examples.

One of the key "soft" skills in sustaining sales excellence is called critical thinking. It is the ability to stop, reflect on what went well, what did not go well, and what you could do better. It is embedded in all the techniques and tools in the framework. The result is that even when the seller and/or sales teams are either not aware of the customer's needs or are unable to reveal those needs, the sales excellence framework is built at each sales stage to double-check the answers by forcing the seller to go backward and forward in time, if you will, and check their actions using customer-facing tools.

Let's see what transpired in this example.

Because the checklist at this stage guided the team to activities that demonstrate how to progress their sale, we applied the scorecard progression tool described in depth in Chapter 8. To demonstrate how

Questions (in order of importance)	Opportunity Status	Score
Who understands your projected Business Outcome, Return on Investment (ROI) & quantified client value?	1 All Decision Makers & Stakeholders understand & believe ROI, Business Outcome & Value	10
What is the Compelling Reason that requires this opportunity MUST close when forecasted?	3 No compelling reason, but customer agrees to work to this month	5
Have you asked the key stakeholders what can STOP our solution being implemented?	4 We know but have not asked client directly	1
Who do you have a strong trusting relationship with?	1 Trusted relationship with Users, Executive Directors and C-Level	10
Who have we agreed the buying process, milestones and timescales with?	1 Have agreed and documented process, milestones & timescales with all decision makers	10
What type of project is our solution attached to?	5 Technology evaluation	4
What is the status of the clients Budget?	2 Sufficient budget is assigned to deal	8
Are you in control of the Buying Criteria or Concept / Technology Proof?	2 Concept/ Technology Proof not needed but buying criteria agreed with Decision Maker	8
What is the status of your solution versus the Competition?	5 Know competition but your solution not confirmed as preferential	2
Where are we with our Negotiation on pricing and terms?	2 Pricing agreed with customer, but contract terms outstanding	8
	TOTAL	63

Figure 11.8 The progression scorecard tool: Example 3

the framework tools ensure the seller dives deep into the reasons for the sale being delayed, or lost, or won, I direct you to Figure 11.8, which is the actual tool used in this example. I have given a fictional name, but the content is the result of a real session with the sales team reflecting on their CRM data taken from the Electricity Generating Renewables Company sales opportunity.

As you can clearly see, the eventual opportunity score of winning the sale was 56 percent, which meant that winning the sale was 50/50 and in danger of being lost or delayed unless action was taken. Over the last 15 years, the results from over 400 sales coaching sessions I have noticed that only when the score is under 70 percent, a delay or problem occurs that blocks progress and eventual sales success. The score had surprised the seller and his team and sharing this statistic with them motivated them to go further back in the sale and apply the tools and techniques in the framework. The seller and his team successfully applied the qualification and discovery techniques and tools described in Chapters 5 and 6 using the face-to-face processes so that the answers to the questions were input into the tools by the potential customer, not by the wishful thinking and interpretation of the seller and the team. That accurate data produced were then input into their CRM and used to ask their AI tool very specific questions about the company and about each executive's key goals and strategies. The proposal was redrafted and presented to all the executive board.

By applying the framework, tools, and techniques that actively involved and engaged executives, they too became involved and took part in the sales process of problem solving. Because the key influencers and decision makers had been fully engaged and involved, the final proposals were so familiar to them that they felt they had written them themselves. The final presentation contained no surprises, special deals, or concessions but merely confirmed what had already been discovered, discussed, and decided. Agreement was quickly reached, the purchase order approved, and the solution delivered and implemented effectively and efficiently. So the seller and his team received their reward and bonus because they had a happy customer, but more importantly, they had now exceeded their sales target by achieving sales excellence.

Used consistently and practiced regularly, this methodology and the skill sets contained in the sales excellence framework will guide every member of the sales team to achieve their desired success. All the tools and techniques are supported by recent research, as well as demonstrated by the examples in each chapter derived from my extensive practical experience leading and coaching thousands of salespeople and hundreds of sales managers. For example, in their excellent book *Insight Selling: Surprising Research on What Sales Winners Do Differently*, Schultz and Doerr quote a happy customer from their buyer research. I think this statement sums up the impact of achieving sales excellence and provides a good and appropriate ending to this chapter: The customer said that the seller's ability to connect with me and provide insights to my business, educate me on new ideas and perspectives, and then coach and collaborate with me on how and what to buy and confirm business value was the key differentiator. By applying the sales excellence framework and the techniques and tools contained in each chapter, you will demonstrate to your potential and existing customers that you are of unique value to them and will be seen as a genuine trusted advisor. Consequently, you will achieve sales excellence and differentiate yourself by delivering predictable, repeatable, consistent results to become a key member of your sales team and be recognized as a top performer by your sales management and senior executives.

Conclusion and Final Thoughts

In the introduction, I said that the interaction between a professional salesperson, multiple stakeholders, and buyers in a business looking to purchase a solution to their business problem is complex and is not a straightforward sequential process. To repeat, sales leaders know that a good solution with a great sales team tends to beat a great solution with a poor sales team. We now know that sales excellence and high performance matter and are the key ingredients in creating a great sales team. I believe that, assuming you have read, downloaded, and practiced the tools and techniques, and applied the framework, then you will have experienced increased success, more revenue, better forecasting, and high-quality pipeline, to name just a few benefits.

Most of the 4,040 attendees in my workshops from 2012 to 2020 gave wonderful feedback. In all, 90 percent strongly agreed or agreed with the following outcomes:

- Changed and improved my sales behavior for the better.
- Helped increase my sales capabilities and learn new sales skills.
- Helped me remain customer focused by aligning each sales step of the sales execution process with how my customers buy.
- Helped guide me from where I am now to where I want to be in the sales execution process.
- Provided me with effective sales tools to help me navigate the essential selling steps and thus progress my deals to close more sales.
- Gave me a checklist method to assess what stage I am at in the sales execution cycle.
- Helped requalify my current opportunities and take effective remedial action.

In 2020, the COVID pandemic hit the world and changed everything. Face-to-face meetings, training, education workshops, and working from the office and place of work stopped. To this day, it is estimated that working from home, where it is possible, is becoming the norm for many professions. Many claim that virtual selling has also become the norm. In Chapter 1, I cited Jeb Blount saying in his book *Virtual Selling* that everything changed due to the global pandemic. Panic set in and social distancing became normal, as did working from home. In a heartbeat, we went from happy hours to virtual happy hours, conferences to virtual conferences, and selling to virtual selling. He concluded that to remain competitive, sales and business professionals were required to shift the way they engaged prospects and customers. In their book *Virtual Selling* by Mike Schultz, Dave Shaby, and Andy Springer, which I also cited in Chapter 1, the authors emphasize that sales professionals can't sell the same way as they did pre-2020. They claim that if you do, you won't achieve the same results. They recommend changing almost everything you did previously. They conclude that to thrive in sales today, it will require a transition to the new world of selling remotely.

However, I am not sure I agree with the authors' somewhat negative deductions that everything has changed. From 2020 to the present, I have continued to coach sales leaders and sales professionals virtually in one-to-one sessions and groups. I then apply the feedback survey questions to each attendee. Overall, 90 percent continued to reaffirm the above seven key outcomes from my coaching and the application of my tools, techniques, and framework. What has changed is that it takes longer to coach and train someone virtually. To succeed, the sessions must be repeated, and online materials must be provided so that the attendees can work and practice in their own time of choosing. Higher education institutions are applying this approach to their teaching and increasing their reach and impact on students.

That is why I offer online links in the Appendix so you the reader can download whatever you require. Therefore, my own experience since 2020 is that the tools, techniques, and frameworks I teach and coach via Zoom and Teams remain just as powerful, if not more so, in today's fast-moving virtual digital world. Many sales enterprises and technology companies, including when I worked at IBM, had been using virtual techniques with customers and colleagues plus flexible working from home for many years. Higher education and training companies have been using virtual training methods and the advantages of the internet for many years. I agree that the impact of the COVID pandemic resulted in virtual interaction exploding in growth and companies like Zoom tripled sales and revenue overnight, but the argument that sales professionals needed to change their sales techniques completely does not hold true. They certainly had to adapt and change to use virtual interaction technology, but the required sales skills and sales techniques did not change.

As the authors in *Virtual Selling* reinforced in both their books, COVID increased dramatically an already fixed and growing trend taking place in the sales profession. Those sellers adding value and using consultative selling of the type contained in the tools, techniques, and frameworks that I have outlined are increasingly successful, regardless of whether it is virtual or face-to-face. Those who do not add value, who too quickly demonstrate their product or service, send pricing and proposals without really engaging and understanding the prospective customer's business remain at risk and are losing their effectiveness and their jobs. To always be aligned with how their customers buy, many sales organizations are rebuilding their sales teams, automating their processes, changing their job functions, applying new administration and CRM systems, incorporating AI, and stating they only need sales professionals who always excel in performance, consistently, reliably, and predictably.

Benjamin Franklin was reported as saying, "tell me and I forget, teach me and I remember, involve me and I learn." Most sales coaching, training, or sales enablement is usually short and intense. After three days, when asked, the attendees only remember about one-third of what they have been taught according to all the research on training and teaching. Franklin's main point is that you must be involved and engaged to learn new skills. This is what we have achieved together in this book. We have applied our eight hard sales skills to real sales opportunities, and we have learned new techniques. We have practiced with real-world examples. We have introduced the eight soft skills. We have learned how to always align ourselves with our buyer by applying the self-coaching sales excellence framework. We have gained sales excellence and now we have the skills to sustain those skills consistently to:

1. Be on quota and achieve targeted revenue.
2. Build quality and high-value pipeline.
3. Identify, quantify, and validate new sales opportunities.
4. Understand the full extent of business problems and their impact on your clients.
5. Define and deliver a solution that meets your clients' desired business outcomes.
6. Gain acceptance and identify actions to progress the sale.
7. Achieve acceptance and agreement with effective mutually beneficial negotiation.
8. Receive a signed contact, implement successfully, and get customer value confirmed.

However, the secret of success is highlighted by an old saying if at first you don't succeed try, try, and try again. Practice, practice, and more practice is the key to success. The lesson to learn is to do it, redo it, learn from mistakes, reflect, and redo again. Keep this book and the digital tools and techniques as your constant reference and continual self-coaching companion. You will experience the joy of learning, and the joy of reaching your full potential, and achieve a level of success in business and in life that might surprise you but will always reward you. Good luck and good selling.

Appendix

Excellence, success, and higher performance are achieved by practice and continued learning before action. Therefore, to encourage you to practice and as a thank you for buying and reading this book, please contact me at tom@salestechnique.com to gain your special one-off discount voucher code that you can use to download *The Sales Excellence Framework* at a special price.

All you need to do is link to my website www.salestechnique.com click on the Resource Centre tab and you will see the Framework containing all the methodologies, tools, and techniques that you can download with the voucher and practice on your live opportunities.

Alternatively, you can choose to download and practice any one of the specific techniques and tools that you think may immediately help you. Figure A.1 is a helpful guide to navigate your way around the sales excellence tools and techniques that you may want to download from my website. Should you also need my personal help, please contact me via email at tom@salestechnique.com.

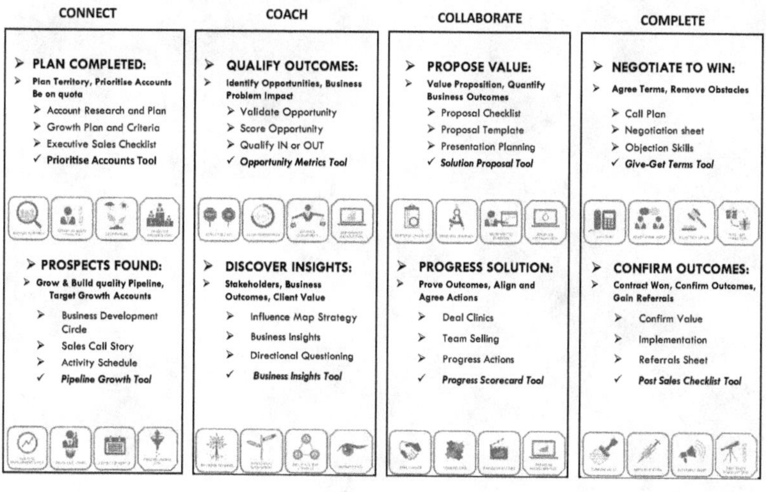

Figure A.1 *Sales excellence framework and program guide. Sales excellence framework, tools, and techniques to download and practice*

References

Chapter 1

1. Tegmark, M. 2017. *Life 3.0: Being Human in the Age of Artificial Intelligence.* Allen Lane.

2. Pink, D.H. 2012. *To Sell is Human: The Surprising Truth About Moving Others.* Riverhead Books.

3. Jefferson, R. 2021. *Sales Enablement 3.0: The Blueprint to Sales Enablement Excellence.* Poppy Court Publishing.

4. Carnegie, D. 2012. *How to Win Friends and Influence People: Special Edition.* Vermillion.

5. Gerstner, Jr, L.V. 2002. *Who Says Elephants Can't Dance: Inside IBM's Historic Turnaround.* HarperCollins.

6. Rodgers, F.G. 'Buck' 1986. *The IBM Way: Insights into the World's Most Successful Marketing Organisation.* Harper and Row.

7. Isaacson, W. 2011. *Steve Jobs: The Exclusive Biography.* Abacus.

8. Shultz, M., D. Shaby, and A. Springer. 2020. *Virtual Selling: How to Build Relationships, Differentiate, and Win Sales Remotely.* Wiley.

9. Weinberg, M. 2018. *New Sales Simplified: The Essential Handbook for Prospecting and New Business Development.* Amacom.

10. Peterson, E., L. Richard. , and R. Timothy. 2011. *Conversations that Win the Complex Sale: Using Power Messaging to Create More Opportunities, Differentiate Your Solutions, and Close More Deals.* McGraw Hill.

11. Dixon, M., and B. Adamson. 2015. *The Challenger Customer: Selling to the Hidden Influencer Who Can Multiply Your Results.* Portfolio Penguin.

12. Schultz, M., and J.E. Doerr. 2014. *Insight Selling: Surprising Research on What Sales Winners Do Differently.* Wiley.

13. Cespedes, F.V. 2014. *Aligning Strategy and Sales: The Choices, Systems, and Behaviours That Drive Effective Selling.* Harvard Business Review.

14. Weinberg, M. 2025. *Sales Truth: Debunk the Myths, Apply Powerful Principles, Win More New Sales.* John Wiley & Sons.

15. *2024 Nobel Prize in Physics.* www.nobelprize.org/prizes/physics/.

16. McLeod, S.A. 2017. *Kolb—Learning Styles.* www.simplypsychology.org/learning-kolb.html.

17. Mazur, E. 2014. *Peer Instruction for Active Learning.* www.youtube.com/watch?v=Z9orbxoRofI.

Bibliography and Suggested Reading List

Important and Relevant to Sales

Bayley, P.D., Bailey, K., Cairns, T., and Grant, S.K. *Seamless: Successful B2B Marketing, Selling, and Account Management*. Business Expert Press, 2023.

Covey, S.R. *The 7 Habits of Highly Effective People*. Simon & Schuster, 1989.

Covey, S.R. *The 8th Habit: From Effectiveness to Greatness*. Simon & Schuster, 2004.

Harari, Y.N. *Sapiens: A Brief History of Humankind*. Penguin Random House UK, 2011.

Tegmark, M. *Life 3.0: Being Human in the Age of Artificial Intelligence*. Allen Lane, 2017.

Active Learning

Anderson, A., and J. Piro. "Conversations in Socrates Café: Scaffolding Critical Thinking via Socratic Questioning and Dialogues." Abstract from *New Horizons for Learning* (NHFL) 11,1 2014.

Barnett, R., and K. Coate. *Engaging the Curriculum in Higher Education*. Maidenhead: Open University Press, 2011.

Harvard Business School. "Inside the Harvard Business School Case Method." 10, 2009. www.youtube.com/watch?v=eA5R41F7d9Q.

Hodge, L., K. Proudford, and H. Holt. "From Periphery to Core: The Increasing Relevance of Experiential Learning in Undergraduate Business Education." *Research in Higher Education* 26 2014.

Kolb, A. Y., and D. A. Kolb. "Learning Styles and Learning Spaces: Enhancing Experiential Learning in Higher Education." *Academy of Management Learning & Education* 4, 2 2005: 193–212.

Laurillard, D. "The Teacher as Action Researcher: Using Technology to Capture Pedagogic Form." *Studies in Higher Education* 33,2 2008: 139–154.

Mazur, E. "Peer Instruction for Active Learning." 18, 2014. www.youtube.com/watch?v=Z9orbxoRofI.

McLeod, S.A. "Kolb—Learning Styles." *Simply Psychology*. 2017. www.simplypsychology.org/learning-kolb.html.

Nicol, D. J., and D. Macfarlane-Dick. "Formative Assessment and Self-Regulated Learning: A Model and Seven Principles of Good Feedback Practice." *Studies in Higher Education* 31,2 2006: 199–218.

Thompson, N., and J. Pascal. "Developing Critically Reflective Practice." *Reflective Practice* 13, 2 2012: 311–325.

Executing Sales

Blount, J. *Virtual Selling: A Quick-Start Guide to Leveraging Video, Technology, and Virtual Communication Channels to Engage Remote Buyers and Close Deals Fast.* Wiley, 2020.

Blount, J. *Fanatical Prospecting: The Ultimate Guide to Opening Sales Conversations and Filling the Pipeline by Leveraging Social Selling, Telephone, Email, Text, and Cold Calling.* Wiley, 2015.

Burg, B., and J.D. Mann. *Go-Givers Sell More.* Penguin Books, 2010.

Caponi, T. *The Transparency Sale: How Unexpected Honesty and Understanding the Buying Brain Can Transform Your Results.* Ideapress Publishing, 2020.

Carnegie, D. *How to Win Friends and Influence People: Special Edition.* Vermilion, 2012.

Cespedes, F.V. *Aligning Strategy and Sales: The Choices, Systems, and Behaviors That Drive Effective Selling.* Harvard Business Review, 2014.

Cespedes, F.V. *Sales Management That Works: How to Sell in a World That Never Stops Changing.* Harvard Business Review, 2021.

Dixon, M., and B. Adamson. *The Challenger Sale: How To Take Control of the Customer Conversation.* Portfolio Penguin, 2013.

Dixon, M., and B. Adamson. *The Challenger Customer: Selling to the Hidden Influencer Who Can Multiply Your Results.* Portfolio Penguin, 2015.

Doerr, J., and M. Schultz. *Rainmaking Conversations: Influence, Persuade, and Sell in Any Situation.* John Wiley & Sons, 2013.

Gerstner, Louis V. Jr. *Who Says Elephants Can't Dance: Inside IBM's Historic Turnaround.* HarperCollins, 2002.

Holland, J.R., and T. Young. *Rethinking the Sales Cycle: How Superior Sellers Embrace the Buying Cycle to Achieve a Sustainable and Competitive Advantage.* McGraw Hill, 2010.

Irving, J. *The B2B Selling Guidebook.* ebookpartnership.com, 2020.

Isaacson, W. *Steve Jobs: The Exclusive Biography.* Abacus, 2011.

Jefferson, R. *Sales Enablement 3.0: The Blueprint to Sales Enablement Excellence.* Poppy Court Publishing, 2021.

Page, R. *Hope is Not a Strategy: The 6 Keys to Winning the Complex Sale.* Nautilus Press, 2002.

Peterson, E., T. Lee, Riesterer, et al. *The Expansion Sale: Four Must-Win Conversations to Keep and Grow Your Customers.* McGraw Hill, 2020.

Peterson, E., T. Lee, Riesterer, T. *Three Value Conversations: How to Create, Elevate, Capture Customer Value at Every Stage of the Long-Lead Sale.* McGraw Hill, 2015.

Peterson, E., T. Lee, Riesterer, T. *Conversations that Win the Complex Sale: Using Power Messaging to Create More Opportunities, Differentiate Your Solutions, and Close More Deals.* McGraw Hill, 2011.

Pink, D.H. *To Sell Is Human: The Surprising Truth About Moving Others.* Riverhead Books, 2012.

Rodgers, F.G. 'Buck.' *The IBM Way: Insights into the World's Most Successful Marketing Organization.* Harper & Row, 1986.

Read, N.A.C., and S. Bistritz. *Selling to the C-Suite: What Every Executive Wants You to Know About Successfully Selling to the Top.* McGraw-Hill Education, 2018.

Schultz, M., D. Shaby, A. Springer. *Virtual Selling: How to Build Relationships, Differentiate, and Win Sales Remotely.* Wiley, 2020.

Schultz, M., and J.E. Doerr. *Insight Selling: Surprising Research on What Sales Winners Do Differently.* Wiley, 2014.

Sinha, P., A. Shastri, and S. Lorimer. *How Generative AI Will Change Sales.* Harvard Business Review, 2023.

Weinberg, M. *New Sales Simplified: The Essential Handbook for Prospecting and New Business Development.* Amacom, 2018.

Weinberg, M. *Sales Truth: Debunk the Myths, Apply Powerful Principles, Win More New Sales.* John Wiley & Sons, 2025.

Effecting Change

Barez-Brown, C. *How to Have Kick-Ass Ideas: Shake Up Your Business, Shake Up Your Life.* Skyhorse Publishing, 2008.

Cialdini, R.B. *Influence: The Psychology of Persuasion.* Harper Business, 2021.

Covey, S.R., and S. Covey. *The 7 Habits of Highly Effective People: Revised and Updated: 30th Anniversary Edition.* Simon & Schuster, 2020.

Collins, J. *How the Mighty Fall: And Why Some Companies Never Give In.* Random House, 2009.

Kotter, J., and H. Rathgeber. *Our Iceberg Is Melting, That's Not How We Do It Here: 2 Books Collection Set.* Macmillan/Portfolio, 2019.

Kotter, J.P. *Leading Change: With a New Preface by the Author.* Harvard Business Review, 2012.

Creating Teamwork

Clayton, E. *Brilliant Teams: The Art and Science of Leading Exceptional Teams.* Authors & Co., 2024.

Dawson, N. *TeamWork: How to Build a High-Performance Team.* Houndstooth Press, 2021.

Druskat, V.A., S.B. Wolf, and P.F. Levy. *Teams That Succeed.* Harvard Business Review, 2005.

Katzenbach, J.R., and D.K. Smith. *The Discipline of Teams.* Harvard Business Review, 2009.

Maginn, M. *Making Teams Work: 24 Lessons for Working Together Successfully.* McGraw Hill, 2004.

About the Author

Tom Cairns loves coaching sales and selling. His mantra is nothing happens in business until something is sold. His driving force in life and business is to help people reach their full potential. To experience the joy of achieving success that you never thought possible. Being excellent in something you care about.

Born in Glasgow from humble beginnings, he graduated in pure science from Glasgow University and joined the fledgling computer industry in the 1970s where he first experienced the rewards of successful sales. Forty years of consistent achievement followed with senior executive positions in multiple global companies including Apple, Wang, Lotus Software, and IBM. Always interested in new technology his entrepreneurial spirit led him to be involved as a founder in a global start-up and to build his own consultancy enterprises.

He believes he is fortunate to have had a successful career in one of the most exciting global industries with leading-edge technology that captured people's imagination and transformed enterprises and society itself. Consequently, his passion is to share the knowledge and skills he has gained, and now spends his time as founder and managing director of SalesTechnique Limited, delivering practical, proven methodologies, tools, and techniques to help sales professionals achieve sales excellence and their desired success.

Tom is a fellow of the Higher Education Academy and Advance HE and is a fully qualified higher education lecturer in learning, teaching, and management education.

Index